Dear Human:

MASTER YOUR EMOTIONS

Volume 1 of The Inner Mastery Series

MARK YOUNGBLOOD

Inspired Forever Books
Dallas, Texas

Dear Human: Master Your Emotions
Volume 1 of The Inner Mastery Series

Copyright © 2017-2021 Mark Youngblood

All rights reserved, including the right of reproduction in whole or in part in any form without prior written permission, except in the case of brief quotations embodied in critical reviews and certain other noncommercial uses permitted by copyright law.

Inspired Forever Books
"Words with Lasting Impact"
Dallas, Texas
(888) 403-2727
https://inspiredforeverbooks.com

Cover design by Rick Rodriguez of Art Republic of Texas

Printed in the United States of America

Library of Congress Control Number: 2014958492

ISBN-13: 978-1-948903-57-8

Dear Human, Master Your Emotions is full of practical insights for understanding the positive role of emotions in your life and harnessing them for your benefit. Youngblood provides innovative strategies for processing your emotions quickly, gently, and easily that are helpful both at work and at home.

— Dr. Marshall Goldsmith, #1 Leadership Thinker, Exec Coach, *New York Times* bestselling author, Dartmouth Tuck Professor of Management Practice

Learning to awaken the ability to reduce reactivity in this hyper-stimulating world is a foundational skill for living that Mark teaches better than anyone I've met.

— Dylan Ratigan, *New York Times* bestselling author and former host of MSNBC's highest-rated daytime TV show, *The Ratigan Show*

"Mark Youngblood takes his readers on an enlightened journey of the human experience. *Dear Human: Master Your Emotions* not only looks at the power of emotions to drive behavior, but how what we focus on engages the Inner State that drives that behavior – consciously or unconsciously. Mark points raise awareness of what it means to live as a Creator and to be at choice, even in the face of the inevitable challenge that comes with the journey."

— David Emerald, Author of *The Power of TED** *(*The Empowerment Dynamic)*

If you purchase one book this year, I recommend *Dear Human, Master Your Emotions*. Mark Youngblood provides clear insights with simple yet powerful strategies for transforming your life by shifting from suppressing to addressing your emotions.

— Joe Duran, CEO, United Capital Financial Advisers and *New York Times* bestselling author of *The Money Code*

Mark Youngblood is a modern day spiritual guru who goes right to the root of any issue and works to release, mend or restore your being. I have worked with him for many years and feel he has help to propel my personal relationships as well as helped me achieve my professional goals and beyond. In *Dear Human, Master Your Emotions*, Mark shares his wisdom and many of his strategies for transforming your life. Read it, follow the guidance, and open the door to a great life!

— Brenda Boone, President & CEO, Human Solutions Inc.

Dear Human, Master Your Emotions, intertwines direct guidance with personal anecdotes. Author Mark Youngblood brings humor and real world strategies to even the most enlightened and self-aware individual. Experience your own personal development journey with this unique book. From new moms to seasoned executives, anyone with a growth mindset can benefit from Mark's guidance. I look forward to the next book in the *Dear Human* series!

— Kristin Horler, Founder and CEO of Baby Boot Camp

Mark's advice is simply presented but profound and life-changing. I've personally experienced how transformative following the courses of action he lays out can be. Everything Mark offers in Dear Human, Meet Your Emotions is actionable and tested by Mark not only by decades of work with his clients but, perhaps more importantly, by practicing himself.

— Jonah Sachs, Founder of Free Range Studios, author of *Winning the Story Wars*

DEDICATION

To all my Teachers who showed me the path
to an awakened life!

ACKNOWLEDGMENTS

I want to acknowledge with deep gratitude the many people and influences that made this book possible. First and foremost, I want to thank Source for the inspiration, wisdom, and resources that enabled me to produce this book. To my beloved wife Rachel, whose encouragement, support, insights, and partnership contributed significantly to this book and to my sheer joy in life. Thank you to my publisher, Michelle Morse, and her team at Inspire On Purpose Publishing. Michelle is a beautiful person and the best partner a writer could ask for in a publisher. I want to acknowledge my dear friend Rand Stagen for his wisdom, guidance, and insights, which helped shape the focus of the book and evolve my thinking. To the innumerable people who have contributed to my evolution over the years and more recently to the crafting and production of this book, thank you! And finally to my readers, thank you for your commitment to making life better for yourself and others and for bringing more Light and Love into the world!

TABLE OF CONTENTS

Introduction: A User's Guide for Your Emotions......1

Part 1. Take Your Life off Autopilot......................7

Chapter 1: You Deserve a Great Life!.........................9
Life Lessons from the Trenches
A Great Life Is Within Your Reach

Chapter 2: We Are Complex People Leading Complex Lives..17
Public Image vs. Private Reality
Behind the Curtain
A Reflection of Your Life

Chapter 3: Claiming Your Power............................27
The Power to Choose
Power Is Not Force
Power Comes from Within

Chapter 4: Drama Is Kryptonite to Your Power.....33
    Emotions Trounce Logic
    The Anatomy of Drama
    The Drama Not-So-Merry-Go-Round
    The Trouble with Villains
    The Antidote to Drama

Chapter 5: Choosing Your Reality............................55
    Reality Is All in Your Head
    Filtering and Distorting Reality
    Stories Govern Our Lives
    Big "T" vs. Little "t" Truth

Chapter 6: Embracing Your Emotions......................71
    Our Struggle with Emotions
    Suppressing "Black Sheep" Emotions
    Thoughts vs. Emotions
    Emotions Are Messengers
    Natural vs. Reactive Emotions

Chapter 7: The High Cost of Avoiding Emotional Pain..83
    The Emotional Roller Coaster
    The Root Cause of Reactions
    Drama Distracts from Pain
    Numbing Through Addictions
    Numbing Through Compulsive Behaviors

TABLE OF CONTENTS

Chapter 8: The Secret for Reprogramming Your Autopilot.............97

The "Parts" of Your Autopilot

Triggers Are Programmed into Your Autopilot

Reprogramming Your Autopilot

Part 2. Create a Great Life............107

Chapter 9: Mindfulness — Laying the Foundation for Power............105

The True Source of Stress

Stress Increases Reactive Behaviors

The Sky-High Cost of Stress

Assessing Your Stress Level

Tracking Your Stress

4 Steps to Manage Your Stress

Creating Focused Awareness

Letting Go of Preoccupations

Chapter 10: Drain the Pain — From Upset to Calm in 60 Seconds............131

How to Drain the Pain

Applying Drain the Pain

Rescuing Yourself from Emotional Hijack

Chapter 11: Empathic Listening — The Healing Power of Empathic Connection........141
An Eventful Dinner with Akeela and Tom
Empathic Listening Is Not "Fixing It"
An Overview of Empathic Listening
What If You Don't Care About Their Feelings?
How to Listen Empathically
Applying Empathic Listening

Chapter 12: Consoling Yourself — Be Your Own Knight in Shining Armor....................161
When Drain the Pain Isn't Enough
How to Console Yourself
Applying the Console Yourself Practice

Chapter 13: Max the Moment — Be Your Best When the "Chips Are Down"............169
Taking the High Road
"Throwing the Switch" to a Creative Response
Overview of Max the Moment
Step 1 — Tame It
Step 2 — Name It
Step 3 — Reframe It

TABLE OF CONTENTS

Chapter 14: Applying Max the Moment...................195

    Example 1 — Missing an Important Meeting

    Example 2 — Trying to Be "Superwoman"... and Failing

    Escaping Your Personal "Ground Hog Day"

    Example 3 — Preventing Recurring Patterns of Behavior

    Overview of Applying Max the Moment

Epilogue: Your Ongoing Journey of Inner Mastery...................217

About the Author...................221

Sources...................223

INTRODUCTION

A User's Guide for Your Emotions

Sometimes it feels like I've spent my whole life trying to figure it all out. In fact, I've often felt like an alien who's learning how to be a human being, and then learning how to cope with other human beings who also seem to be trying to figure it all out. At times, it's been pretty difficult!

I've dedicated decades trying to understand what it takes to lead a successful and fulfilling life. One of my greatest lessons learned has been this: the power to change our world—to make it what we want—exists within each of us.

As an executive coach and Inner Mastery teacher and facilitator, I've also learned that with the right knowledge and skills, making those changes can actually be fast and easy. I wasn't expecting that. I was taught change is hard ... Weren't you?

True fulfillment comes when you change what happens inside of you while you live in this complex and chaotic world just the way it is.

Through my work in the business and private sectors, I have seen first-hand how many people are leading lives of "not-so-quiet desperation." We're all looking for solutions for a better life. Unfortunately, nothing we've found seems to last.

This search for happiness leads millions of people to look for answers "out there." They believe they would be happy if they could just have

- more money,
- more power,
- a better body,
- a different boss or new job,
- a cool car or designer clothes, or
- the newest gadget.

Or maybe if

- their partner loved them more,
- their children did as they were told,
- somebody would help out around the house, or
- they could go on the vacation they've always wanted … maybe that would do the trick.

I'm sure you have noticed the world "out there" rarely cooperates with your wishes. Let's face it; the world doesn't much care about your happiness. Sure, there are some things you can change, but most of your life conditions are out of your control.

You simply cannot control the world. Your efforts to do so will likely exhaust you and create even more unhappiness. Even if you obtained everything you wanted—or

INTRODUCTION

became a multi-millionaire—it still wouldn't guarantee lasting happiness.

True fulfillment comes when you change what happens *inside of you* while you continue to live in this complex and chaotic world *just the way it is*. It involves learning to live in a *new way*, with a *new level of consciousness*.

You can't change THE world, but you *can* change YOUR world.

To paraphrase Albert Einstein, "You can't change your life with the same consciousness you used to create it." If you truly want to change your world, you must start with the person in the mirror.

Your journey begins by developing a new relationship with your emotions. Each of us is born with a colorful palette of emotions, but somebody made a colossal mistake by forgetting to give us a user manual! We've been left to our own devices to figure out what to do with our emotions, and frankly, most of us have made a mess of it.

> You can't change THE world, but you can change YOUR world.

The purpose of this book is to provide you with a user-friendly guide to your emotions. My goal is to help you gain greater understanding and acceptance of your emotions by imparting powerful life skills that will allow you to take charge of them.

Emotional reactions often lead to drama and negative consequences for those involved. Through Inner Mastery, you will be able to manage your emotions effectively and opt out of the drama to allow for positive outcomes for everyone.

You create your world from the inside out. Through Inner Mastery, you can

- remain calm and centered,
- reduce and even eliminate your drama and upsets,
- be happier,
- be more successful,
- improve your health,
- create loving relationships, and
- find fulfillment in your life.

The primary objective is to stop *reacting to life* and start *creating the life you want*.

This book has been divided into two parts to help you process, and put into practice, the life changes necessary for creating a fulfilling life.

Part 1. Take Your Life off Autopilot

Together, we will explore how you create your life experience through "drama stories"—the ways in which you think about and process situations—which are largely the source of your stress, upsets, and unhappiness. We'll examine your use of power and force and the consequences each one creates; consider ways you can restore from your subconscious "autopilot" the authority to choose your thoughts, emotions, and behaviors; and delve deeper into understanding your emotions and the source of your emotional reactions. As we do this, I will point out the many consequences you might experience

INTRODUCTION

by avoiding emotional pain. And finally, I'll reveal the secret for reprogramming your autopilot and restoring your power to choose the life you want.

Part 2. Create a Great Life

The last half of the book is devoted to practical life skills you can employ to create a great life. You will discover how to quickly and easily shift from a reactive to a creative response. You will explore how mindfulness reduces your stress and quiets your mind. You'll learn about the Drain the Pain and Consoling Yourself life skills, which will allow you to easily release suppressed emotions and drain the charge from drama. You'll discover how the Empathic Listening life skill enables you to help other people gently move through their emotional upsets. And you'll be introduced to the powerful 3-Step Max the Moment practice for pivoting to power, which concludes this section.

Throughout, examples have been drawn from my own personal experiences and those of my clients. Unless otherwise indicated, names and key aspects of the stories have been altered to preserve anonymity. To provide continuity through the book, I introduce a fictional family who represents a composite of many of the clients and their families I've worked with and helped over the past two decades: Akeela and Tom Lewis and their children Zuri, Sophie, and James.

Through the Lewis family, we address business and leadership challenges as well as family, relationship, and personal issues. Hopefully, you will be able to relate their stories to your own life and the lives of those you love.

I hope the ideas that you glean from these pages will help you to live a rich and fulfilling life, and to be your best self every day!

Mark Youngblood

PART 1

Take Your Life off Autopilot

CHAPTER 1

You Deserve a Great Life!

Everyone wants a great life—to be happy, successful, and fulfilled. Don't you?

I'm sure there are times when you feel like all is well in the world and life is good. But in between those times, life doesn't always seem so great. As the saying goes, "Sometimes you are the windshield and sometimes you are the bug." Have you ever felt that way? I know I have.

It probably isn't a revelation to you that society is in crisis. I could fill this entire chapter with research, statistics, and stories about how sick, upset, stressed, depressed, overworked, sleep deprived, insecure, fearful, unappreciated, unloved, and unfulfilled most people are. But what would be the point? You already know that.

> *Imagine a life where you are able to be your Best Self every day, all the time!*

Life doesn't have to be that way. What if you had the power to transform your world and to do so in a surprisingly short period of time?

Imagine a life where you could be your best self every day, all the time. Where almost everything that upsets you no longer bothered you. Where you felt

- loved and appreciated, and
- you no longer obsessed over anxieties and worries.

A life where you could make it through your day—the same kind of day you currently have

- feeling relaxed, energized, and satisfied,
- no longer carrying anger, resentment, or hurt from your past upsets and heartbreaks, and
- truly feeling joy and fulfillment every day.

As "pie-in-the-sky" as that sounds, you can have all that and much more. But there is a catch … *you* have the starring role in creating this scenario for yourself.

I know, because I've been there, and I'm speaking from personal experience. This book is written from the down-and-dirty trenches of real emotions, relationships, and challenging life circumstances. I ultimately learned how to master my emotions because I was making a mess of my life and I desperately needed to do something to turn it around.

Life Lessons from the Trenches

I am passionate and emotional and always have been. I was a loving, affectionate, and expressive child, but was also prone to emotional storms. My childhood temper

CHAPTER 1

tantrums were the stuff of legends! Unfortunately, it didn't take long for my emotional outbursts to get me in trouble, which was bad news in our household.

My father was an enthusiastic practitioner of the "spare the rod, spoil the child" school of parenting. I endured a lot of whippings that bordered on beatings. Afterwards, my father would tell me to stop crying or he would give me another whipping. And you'd better believe I did! Then he would say, "Now come here and give me a hug." Imagine the emotional confusion I internalized from those mixed messages!

> *Stop reacting to life and start creating the life you want.*

Punishment was meted out unpredictably for something as simple as knocking over my milk or as serious as running away from home, which I tried to do when I was 5 years old.

At times, all of us kids would be punished even if only one of us committed a "crime." My father reasoned that we probably did something wrong, he just didn't know what yet. I lived in nearly constant fear and learned at an early age how to "walk on eggshells."

My father was not a villain, and in many respects, his essential goodness showed through his generosity and many acts of service. As a Boy Scout troop leader, he shepherded three sons through the rank of Eagle Scout. He led his troop on countless monthly campouts, annual summer camps, two national jamborees, Philmont Scout Ranch, and a 50-mile boat trip down the turgid waters of southeast Texas. He was awarded the Silver Beaver Medal—one of scouting's highest honors—for his many years of service. Scouts from his troop dropped by the house to see him for years after he quit scouting, and several paid their respects at his funeral nearly 50 years after he had served as their scoutmaster.

Looking back, I realize he had scarcely more emotional maturity than his 2-year-old son. I learned later about his childhood, and it made mine seem like a catered picnic in the park. I believe my father had been a tender-hearted boy who was traumatized early and often. He hardened his heart to survive—like so many people do—and it eventually killed him. He struggled with his own emotional demons, and I think he subconsciously unleashed them on his children. He tried to chase them away with alcohol and hard work, but I fear they pursued him to the grave.

So, I learned to be a good boy—a self-proclaimed "golden boy"—or at least to pretend to be one. However, my emotions continued to rage inside me. I would receive good citizen awards at school and bully my little sister at home.

Gaining a new and healthier relationship with your emotions will transform your life for the better in almost every possible way!

As a young adult, I was an emotional mess. I learned to mask my emotions, but they didn't stay suppressed for long. I was charming, friendly, insightful, witty, and wicked smart. I was also cocky, arrogant, thin-skinned, and carried a great big chip on my shoulder. I defended my fragile ego through sarcasm, criticism, and a rapier-sharp tongue. I craved love and affection, but feared in my heart I was despicable. All of which made me insecure, needy, self-centered, and self-loathing.

CHAPTER 1

In my 20s, I had three consecutive wake-up calls.

First, my boss told me he would never put me in front of senior executives because I was "a loose cannon," and he was afraid of what I might say. My ambition wouldn't tolerate that. So I took advantage of every self-development and management training available. I proved my old boss wrong when I became one of the youngest people the accounting department ever promoted to management.

But all that development wasn't enough to save my first marriage, which lasted less than two years. I was hopelessly ill-equipped for the emotional demands of a committed relationship, and failed miserably. At the time, I was still clinging to my fragile identity as "the golden boy," and divorce proved to be a cruel blow.

At age 28, my wounded ego suffered a coup de grâce.

The failure of my ill-fated entrepreneurial venture, MortgageNet, was the third strike. I masked a deep insecurity with hubris and over-confidence. I placed all my eggs in this basket and they were quickly scrambled. I needed the business to succeed in order to prove my worth. I had visions of being a millionaire, and imagined how I would be admired once I had achieved such success. But I didn't really know what I was getting into, and so the business was doomed from the start.

One day, I realized all my savings were gone and I had funds for about two more weeks. With no prospects for income in sight, I ran out of time.

The nearly simultaneous collapse of my marriage and company led to an "ego death." The false facade of my self-image collapsed under the combined weight of my failures. I was in agony ... it felt like the end of my world.

But there was a blessing waiting for me. In the dark depths of my emotional torment, I had a blinding mystical vision. This led to a spiritual renaissance and a profound commitment to Inner Mastery and spiritual growth, which I pursue to this day.

Since then, I have had other challenges and setbacks, both professionally and personally. However, I turned them into a master class for my emotional healing and personal growth. And for that reason, I am deeply grateful for those trials and hardships.

I'm now reaping the benefits of all that hard work and emotional healing. My company, Inner Mastery, Inc., is celebrating nearly 25 years. I am married to a beautiful and amazing woman. We share a love and a joyful companionship most people dream of having. Make no mistake; we have conflicts and challenges like any other couple. But because we share the mindsets and life skills included in this book, we leverage our upsets to heal and draw even closer. We create more intimacy and love with each challenge we face together.

The perspectives and life skills I share with you here embody the accumulated lessons from my personal school of hard knocks. I want to share what I have learned so you can enjoy a great life too, and hopefully achieve it more gently and easily than I did!

A Great Life Is Within Your Reach

Historically, people have devoted their entire lifetimes to achieving the peace, love, and fulfillment you seek.

CHAPTER 1

Fortunately, there have been extraordinary advances in transformational practices that have dramatically shortened the time required. With the mindsets and proven strategies you will discover in these pages, you will be able to see immediate, positive results in your quality of life. With steady practice, you can profoundly transform your life in as little as a year or two.

Certainly these are bold—even outrageous—assertions about how great your life can be. If you are a little bit skeptical, well you're justified. I don't expect you to trust my word on it; just read on and try my recommendations for yourself and let your results speak for themselves.

Emotions live at the heart of Inner Mastery. We are emotional beings and our emotions have a profound effect on our individual and societal health and well-being. Gaining a new and healthier relationship with your emotions will transform your life for the better in almost every possible way:

- improved health
- more loving and positive relationships
- greater success in business
- more peace and contentment
- more joy and fulfillment

I have transformed my own life through the strategies I am sharing here with you. I know what it's like to go from wanting to escape an unhappy and unfulfilling life to embracing an enriched one of joy and fulfillment. And I'm not the only one.

The people I have worked with and helped over the years in both the business world and private sector have experienced similar results.

Leadership coaching with senior-level executives is the mainstay of my work, and Inner Mastery is a major part of my year-long Exceptional Leader Coaching Program™. My clients include some of the most successful people in business. They are no-nonsense, get-it-done type women and men with little tolerance for anything that wastes their time. They wouldn't engage in these materials if they didn't achieve such profound results.

> We are emotional beings and our emotions have a profound effect on our individual and societal health and well-being.

The practices they have learned in my program make them dramatically better leaders, but equally benefit their home lives. In addition to better relationships with their spouse and children, most have found that their health improves and they relax and enjoy life to a much greater degree.

People in the private sector who discovered Inner Mastery through classroom programs or individual life coaching achieved similar life-changing results. I am confident you can too!

CHAPTER 2

We Are Complex People Leading Complex Lives

When I first met Akeela Lewis, she seemed to be living the American dream.

Akeela is the vice president of customer success in a large technology company, Techmore Products, Inc., and a rising star in her industry. She is trim and fit and looks much younger than her 38 years. She is a self-described fitness nut who works out three times per week without fail, eats right, and does yoga just about every day.

She describes herself as happily married and an active and involved mother to her three children. Her oldest, Zuri, is her husband Tom's daughter by another marriage. Akeela began helping to raise Zuri when she was 3 years old; she treats her like her own daughter. Zuri is now 22 and recently graduated from college. Akeela's only son, James, is 15 years old and in high school. James is a musical prodigy who began playing piano when he was only 5 years old. Her youngest daughter, Sophie, just started high school. She is quite popular in school and plays for an elite soccer team.

Based on her description, Akeela is incredibly happy and successful. She has a great job, great health, a happy family, and a bright future. But as I dug deeper, I heard a far different story.

Public Image vs. Private Reality

In my line of work, I often see the stark difference between the public image people present and the private reality of their lives. People work hard to conceal the emotional messiness of their real lives, but that false image comes with a high price tag. That's the way it is with many people—maybe even most of us—and the same holds true for the Lewis family.

I met Akeela through my role as her executive coach. The CEO of her company, Vijay "Jay" Singh, felt that Akeela had a lot of great skills and qualities but he wanted her to achieve her full potential. He recently turned her down for a promotion to the senior vice president position for the sales division. Jay explained that Akeela seemed to lack the maturity and experience necessary to continue her rise in the company. Although Akeela is a star in the organization, some of the rough spots in her interpersonal and leadership styles were creating problems.

Instead, Jay had hired an outsider named Ben Gomez. Akeela believes Ben is less qualified than she and is unhappy about not getting the promotion. She believes she has more than earned this promotion and is still stewing over the situation months later.

CHAPTER 2

The CEO described Akeela in glowing terms, as a capable leader with the potential to step into his job someday. He further explained, "Akeela is friendly, likable, smart and knowledgeable, devoted to her employees, and has a great way with customers. She is a visionary and an inspiring leader, and is known for her creativity in solving tough problems. To many of our most important customers, she is the face of the company and they love her. That is great for our brand. She is a real asset and I want to ensure she has a great future with Techmore."

However, according to Jay, Akeela also displays some behaviors that need to change. He explained that she could be adamant and inflexible about her point of view, cut people off when they were talking, and came across as arrogant and critical at times. Her employees love her, but they are also frustrated with her. At times, she micromanages her team in the name of "helping out," overrides their decisions, and tells them how to do their jobs. Her peers complain she is over-protective and defensive when anyone criticizes her team, the organization, or her personally.

> *People work extremely hard to conceal the emotional messiness of their real lives. And that false image comes with a high price tag.*

In addition, Jay feels she is overloading herself with work and some important matters are not being handled on a timely basis. He is worried Akeela is burning herself out. Finally, there are some family issues that are starting to affect her work performance.

It may be a surprise to you that emotions—or rather the ineffective handling of emotions—are at the heart of all of these behavioral issues.

Behind the Curtain

As we began our coaching, Akeela described her background, work situation, and home life. That's when I started to hear the many ways Akeela felt anxious, frustrated, angry, and resentful. She also felt overwhelmed and exhausted from all the stress and burden of her responsibilities at work and home. Like millions of smart, responsible women, she felt she had to be perfect and to be everything to everyone. It was all becoming too much for her. Have you ever felt that way?

Akeela described her background, "I have always been super responsible, going back to when I was a child. With two working parents and the oldest of four children, I found myself in the unwanted and thankless role of caring for my siblings. I kept that role throughout my high school years, even though it meant missing out on many of the fun experiences my friends were able to enjoy."

Even though she was better than average in most things she did, her younger brother "could do no wrong." He was a star athlete and top student and was popular in school. Akeela grew up in his shadow and felt like she always had to work twice as hard to get half the recognition he received without even trying.

Her strong work ethic and resentment over feeling unacknowledged has stayed with her to this day. As you will discover later, these emotional experiences from our childhood create our reactionary behaviors. These experiences get programmed into your subconscious, and then your autopilot replays them from that point on. Akeela's life-long pattern of reacting with resentment was causing

CHAPTER 2

her to have "a chip on her shoulder" at work and to take offense even when none was intended.

On the other hand, there are often positive benefits to the emotional traumas we experience as well. For instance, these same factors drove Akeela to earn scholarships to attend college and obtain grants and loans for the remainder of the tuition. In her career, she started at the bottom in her company, but through drive and determination, she blazed her way to the top of the organization.

Many people in top management positions have stories similar to Akeela's. They overcame emotional traumas, which provided the tenacity and drive to rise to the top. I know executives who

- grew up in a war zone,
- suffered the death of a parent when they were young children,
- had fist fights with their drunken father,
- grew up in abject poverty and lack,
- survived rioting, which killed people just outside their home,
- grew up in alcoholic or abusive households,
- were sexually molested, or
- were bullied in school.

And the list goes on. These people heroically triumphed over the adversity of their childhood. Unfortunately, these events also produced deep-seated insecurities, which tend to show up as undesirable behaviors, just as what was now happening with Akeela.

It doesn't take a major trauma to create emotional insecurities that extend from childhood into our lives as adults. Most people don't experience major traumas like those described above. But to a child, even a seemingly small incident might be emotionally devastating. These incidents might include a parent

- breaking a promise to them,
- not comforting them when they were upset and crying,
- saying a cross word at the wrong time, or
- embarrassing or shaming them in front of others.

There are an infinite number of ways we develop emotional wounds that carry over into adulthood. Yours are unique to you.

Akeela feels like her life is falling apart and an avalanche of unfair circumstances is cascading down on her. She complains she is being penalized as a woman for behaviors men, including the CEO, exhibit as well. These behaviors are unjustly described as "too strong" when they come from her. She is frustrated with her team for being so needy and demanding. She feels she gives so much to her job and yet she receives insufficient appreciation for everything she does.

Troubles in Akeela's home life contribute tremendously to her stress. Her husband lost his job six months earlier and is not taking it well. Tom was a successful VP of marketing for a manufacturing company but was laid off when construction declined. Making matters worse, they had just bought a new "mini-mansion" and now money is an everyday concern.

CHAPTER 2

Tom's attempts to find a new job have come up empty, which is a major blow to his self-esteem. He feels ashamed and those feelings grow worse every day he is unemployed. Tom adopted the role of house husband and "soccer dad" when they could no longer afford the nanny. The kids never had much time with him before because he was a workaholic. They are not adapting well to him constantly being around. He runs the household like he ran his team in business—barking out orders and being a perfectionist. This is further alienating the children.

He also tries to tell Akeela how to do her job. As you might guess, this is a growing source of friction. Tom is diligent about getting the kids to their events and activities but feels humiliated hanging out with all the stay-at-home mothers. Tom's anger and resentment continues to build each day. Then he takes it out on the kids and his wife.

> *Every family's story has ups and downs, successes and failures, fun times and hard times. There is love and there is conflict. That's the way of life.*

Akeela's children are sources of both joy and heartache. She is loving and attentive toward them and is proud of them and often says so. But she also worries about them. James is a gentle and sensitive teenager who is overweight and a total failure at sports. He was always plump but has started gaining more weight and has recently been diagnosed as pre-diabetic. The school kids bully him for being "fat" and accuse him of being gay. That's bad enough, but to further complicate matters, his own father also fears James is gay. Tom constantly pushes him to "be more manly." Tom's attempts to engage James in sports were disastrous. As a result of all these factors,

James has retreated into his own world—hiding in his room and immersing himself in music and video games.

Akeela's daughter Sophie is an elite soccer player but plays two other sports well. Tom pressures her to focus on soccer so she can get a scholarship. But Sophie actually prefers softball. She is becoming burned out by all the sports practice and the demands on her time severely limit her social activities. Lately, she has been acting out both at school and at home. She remains close with Akeela but fights with her father almost every day.

Like many young adults in her generation, Zuri just feels lost. Akeela's oldest daughter graduated from a prestigious university with a 4.0 GPA and $40,000 in college debt. Since receiving her diploma a year ago, she has been on exactly two job interviews. Neither panned out. All of this occurred despite having a degree in marine biology and volunteering regularly at the local marine aquarium.

> *If you are waiting for the world to change so you can be happy, you are going to be waiting forever. The world isn't going to change just for you.*

Zuri is working part-time hourly jobs while she looks for permanent employment, and she hates it. But at least she is out of the house and away from her father. Tom rides her constantly about not working hard enough or showing enough determination to "get out and get a real job." Zuri believes Tom is being hypercritical given his own inability to land a job. And now Zuri is talking about giving up on marine biology, which she loves.

Akeela worries Zuri is becoming depressed.

CHAPTER 2

Of course the positives in their lives tend to balance out these difficulties. All of Akeela's children experience success and have activities they love doing and are good at. They have family dinners every Monday night. Everyone seems to enjoy this family ritual, at least until recently. Their family vacation the prior summer reminded Akeela of the happier times as a family. She wishes those feelings would last.

A Reflection of Your Life

Akeela's story is a lot like every family's story. There are ups and downs, successes and failures, fun times and hard times. There is love and there is conflict. That's the way of life.

We all constantly face one challenge or another and the "good times" never seem to last. We experience tough situations at work, struggles in our love relationships, difficulties with our children, and concerns about how they are doing. We worry about aging parents, lots of college debt with no job opportunities, and walking through life with no clear purpose. All these conditions lead to stress and unhappiness—the opposite of what we actually want. Do any of these challenges sound familiar to you?

You can *seem* to have it all, like Akeela, and still spend most of your time upset, stressed, and unhappy. You dream of life getting better, of getting past the difficulties and hard times … as if there will ever be such a time.

Akeela wanted

- her promotion and the people at work to appreciate her more.
- her husband to get a job and quit being a jerk to her and the kids.
- Zuri to find a job in the career of her choice.
- James to lose weight, improve his health, and for kids to be nice to him.
- Sophie to be able to focus on and enjoy the sport she loves.

If all that happened, Akeela was sure her life would be great. What circumstances would you like to change that you think would make your life much better?

What I told Akeela in our first meeting is an important example of what I intend to demonstrate to you throughout this book: if you are waiting for the world to change so you can be happy, you are going to be waiting forever.

You can be happy and fulfilled when you accept the world the way it is—complex, difficult, and chaotic—and where things often don't turn out the way you want.

The world isn't going to change just for you. You can, however, be content and fulfilled when you embrace the world the way it is—complex, difficult, and chaotic—and accept the fact that things often don't turn out the way you want.

The key to doing this is to develop Inner Mastery, which includes the ability to manage your emotions and transform the drama in your life. Fortunately, you have the power within you to change your world and achieve the contentment, success, and fulfillment you are craving.

CHAPTER 3

Claiming Your Power

When you accept responsibility for something you did wrong rather than defending yourself or blaming others, that's power. When your children are tussling and accidentally break an expensive lamp, and you respond to the situation in a calm way rather than yelling at or hitting them, that's power. When you are almost sideswiped by a driver veering across your lane in traffic and you pray for them to make it home safely rather than cursing at them, that's power. When you believe in something and stand up for that belief even when it is unpopular with others, that's power.

You can think of "power" as the ability to *choose a positive response to a situation which achieves mutually beneficial outcomes.*

The Power to Choose

There are many things we cannot choose in our lives, things that are beyond our ability to control and influence.

For example:

- we are born with certain body shapes, skin colors, capabilities, and limitations
- in families we didn't choose
- with parenting styles we didn't get to vote on
- were abused by people we trusted
- were in accidents we didn't create
- suffered discrimination that wasn't fair or deserved

However, everyone has the option to *choose what you will think and how you will behave*—essentially, who you will *be* in any given situation. You may not want the negative things that happened to you in your life, or maybe are still happening to you. But you can choose how you are going to respond—what you are going to make of that situation and ultimately of your life.

> You have the option to choose what you will think and how you will behave — essentially, who you will be in any given situation.

Viktor Frankl was a death camp survivor of the Nazi holocaust during World War II who went on to become a prominent psychiatrist. His book *Man's Search for Meaning* is a poignant tribute to the triumph of the human spirit over even the worst of circumstances. Frankl observed that the majority of the prisoners believed they were victims of fate with no power over their lives—no choice over their actions. As a result, many "acted like animals" in the single-minded interest of their own preservation. But a rare few did not. These people rose above their circumstances, choosing a different course of action—one of love and service. Frankl wrote of these people:

> *We who lived in concentration camps can remember the men who walked through the huts comforting others, giving away their last piece of bread. They may have been few in number, but they offer sufficient proof that everything can be taken from a man but one thing: the last of the human freedoms—to choose one's attitude in any given set of circumstances, to choose one's own way.*

People can be victims of circumstances, as Frankl was, but they do not have to be victims in light of their thoughts and choice of behaviors. If regular people, just like you and me, can choose deeply loving and humanitarian actions in the face of horrid persecution such as that which Frankl lived through, imagine what is possible for the rest of us faced with the relatively minor issues in our lives!

Power Is Not Force

"Power" is not the same thing as "force." Although they both channel energy to produce a result, power produces positive outcomes for all while force benefits some and damages or penalizes others.

For our purposes, let's define force as overwhelming something or someone against its will or counter to its nature to achieve a desired result. Force often involves reacting to a challenge or need with domination and aggression. This doesn't just refer to obvious attacking-type or combative behaviors. Passive behaviors can feel like an attack as well, as anyone who has ever been subjected to the "silent treatment" or "cold shoulder" can attest. Force involves getting what you want with little regard to the consequences to others—people, society, animals, the environment, or even inanimate objects.

An old friend taught me: "If you have to force it, something's wrong." If you:

- force a screw into a hole, you can strip its threads.
- force yourself to go without adequate sleep for too long, you are going to damage your ability to function effectively, and ultimately affect your health.
- force your will on someone else, you can severely damage the relationship.
- attack someone verbally or physically through action or even inaction, you are going to injure that person psychologically and emotionally.

Using force to get your outcome nearly always leads to damage of some kind, which results in negative long-term consequences.

If you have to force it, something's wrong.

In the Victor Frankl example, the compassionate inmates demonstrated power, and the Nazis were exerting force.

The use of force is behind most harmful things in our world. Of course, there are legitimate times when force is necessary. The primary justification is to protect someone from harm, such as stopping your child from darting out into a busy roadway. I suggest the real need for force is actually quite rare. I encourage you to treat the use of force as a last resort.

Power Comes from Within

Power springs from within you—it is a creative energy fueled by a desire to create some positive outcome. Power brings about positive change without intent to harm.

Consider the power Gandhi, Martin Luther King, Mother Theresa, and even celebrities such as Oprah Winfrey have exercised, and the common good that resulted. Bill W. and Dr. Bob, founders of Alcoholics Anonymous, have contributed to healing countless addicts through their 12-Step program—a masterful use of positive power rather than force. These are merely the tiniest fraction of examples of true power at work in the world.

> You can learn to tap into your power to improve your life and change your corner of the world for the better.

These people have accomplished great things without resorting to force. Instead, they relied on their inner power to create positive change in the world. You have that same source of power within you. You can learn to tap into your power to improve your life and change your corner of the world for the better!

CHAPTER 4

Drama Is Kryptonite to Your Power

Being powerful can also be described as being *resourceful*. According to one definition, being resourceful is "the ability to deal skillfully and promptly with new situations and difficulties." Being resourceful enables you to meet life's challenges in a manner that generates positive outcomes not only for you, but also for any others involved.

Your inner and outer resources enable you to be successful. Outer resources are money, transportation, relationships, equipment, and the like. We will focus on *inner* resources, because in life, the inner creates the outer.

Inner resources include, among other things:

- your knowledge and experience
- skills and capabilities
- positive mindsets and intentions
- intelligence (IQ) and emotional mastery (EQ)
- the ability to manage relationships

- resilience
- faith
- compassion
- ethics and responsibility

Like most people, Akeela has a well-developed set of inner and outer resources. She has used those resources effectively to create a pretty successful life at work and at home.

But notice what happens to Akeela when things get tough—when life doesn't unfold the way she wants. When that happens, she reacts in unproductive ways. When she didn't get the job she wanted, she became angry, resentful, and critical. Then she resisted the leadership of her new boss. When her husband acted poorly, she became frustrated, resentful, and intolerant. Then she criticized and judged him. When her employees didn't perform to her standards, she became impatient, jumped in and micro-managed, and didn't listen to their feedback. All these behaviors are versions of *reacting*.

Obviously, Akeela doesn't react in that manner all the time. Most of the time, she has access to all of her resources, and she meets challenges and difficulties effectively with positive outcomes for all involved. It is only when she is "triggered" emotionally by a situation that she acts in a much less resourceful manner. That's true of most people.

Under challenging circumstances, she loses her access to power and resorts to using force. This illustrates the difference between being a "creator" who uses power and a "reactor" who uses force.

CHAPTER 4

Don't draw the false conclusion that Akeela's reactions are based on her being female. Every human alive has emotional reactions throughout the day, every single day.

Many people live in denial of their emotions. For instance, I often hear statements like, "I'm not emotional, I'm just angry," or "frustrated," or "annoyed," or "stressed." Somehow they don't realize all those things are emotions too. We can be almost blind when it comes to observing and noticing our own emotions because we're so accustomed to constantly living inside of them. Like a fish in the ocean, we can't see the water (emotions) we are swimming in.

Even people who don't visibly show their emotions are still having emotional reactions. They can't help it. If they have a brain, they have emotional reactions.

Emotions Trounce Logic

Human beings are emotional before they are logical. The limbic system—the part of the brain responsible for emotions—leaps into action chemically "light years" before the neocortex (the source of logic) gets involved. Our brains take about 100 milliseconds to react emotionally and about 600 milliseconds for our neocortex to register this reaction. By then, the damage is done. The subconscious autopilot has already jumped in to handle the situation, and voilà, you are reacting. Although everybody has emotional reactions, not everybody acts on them in negative or unproductive ways.

Human beings are emotional before they are logical.

Many people, and especially men, claim to be logical and unemotional in emotionally charged situations. And on the surface, that's what it sometimes looks like. But the revealing factor is *how the logic is being used and to what end.*

If the logic is being used in a *defensive manner*, then the logic is merely an expression of someone's personal emotional reaction.

Defensive logic is used to

- avoid blame,
- shift responsibility,
- invalidate the other person's point of view,
- win,
- be right, and
- dominate the other person and make them feel confused and foolish.

I know this behavior quite well. Early in my life I used it frequently, and it cost me my first marriage. When my wife and I argued, she would become visibly upset. I sought to remain cool, calm, and rational. No matter what she said, I could find the flaws in her argument and counter it. She grew angrier and more frustrated the longer we talked. Finally, she would break down into tears and run to another room and close the door. I viewed that as winning the argument. But, in actuality, we both lost.

> When logic is being used in a defensive manner, it is merely a different kind of expression of an emotional reaction.

CHAPTER 4

The hard truth is this: I was terrified of making a mistake, of doing something wrong. I was having a massive reaction; I just walled it off and tried to avoid letting it show. I desperately needed to avoid being blamed, so I used logic to achieve that goal. That is a classic reactive behavior and a definite use of force.

In contrast, healthy use of logic is

- grounded in humility,
- promotes a greater understanding of the issue,
- validates the other party,
- seeks mutually beneficial outcomes, and
- supports both the health of the relationship and the well-being of the other party.

When you become emotionally reactive, you lose your power. You lose your resourcefulness.

In this way, drama is like Kryptonite. When Superman is exposed to Kryptonite, he grows weak and loses his power. The same thing occurs when you engage in drama. You lose your power and hastily react. As a result, you become weak and lose your ability to produce positive, mutually beneficial outcomes. Then you resort to force and create some measure of harm, even when it appears as if you achieved an outcome you wanted. Just like with my negative use of logic in the marital example above.

Drama can be quite entertaining on TV shows and movies. But it is harmful and potentially devastating in real life.

Even the small dramas you encounter during the course of a typical day take their toll on your well-being. Minor dramas like the weather turning bad, traffic stalling, the wait staff getting your lunch order wrong, someone not responding to your "hello" in the morning, your child missing her ride to school—all of these small dramas add up quickly and can have a significant impact simply because there are so many of them.

> *Drama is to you what Kryptonite is to Superman!*

The Anatomy of Drama

Dr. Steven Karpman developed the Drama Triangle in the late 1960s while studying under Dr. Eric Berne, the father of transactional analysis (TA) psychotherapy. The drama triangle is a simple concept with a profound impact.

In my experience, drama results when you have been *thwarted, threatened,* or *hurt*.

- You have been *thwarted* when something doesn't go your way—some desire, goal, value, wish, hope, or expectation is blocked.
- *Threats* occur when the potential for punishment or injury is made contingent on what you do or don't do, say, think, or feel.
- *Hurt* occurs when you perceive you have suffered some harm—physically, psychologically, or emotionally.

CHAPTER 4

Let's start with a simple example:

Renee, the boss, announces to the project team at four in the afternoon, "Everyone must work late this evening because the project is running behind—no exceptions." Terry becomes furious because he must miss his seven-year-old daughter's ballet recital. He promised her he would come watch her perform and has already missed the previous two performances. He and his teammates spend the next half hour complaining about the boss and the company before reluctantly returning to work.

This is a typical drama story, where "somebody (or something) done somebody else wrong."

You can change the names and details about who did what to whom, but this is essentially the same pattern of reactions most folks engage in every day. To see what I mean, let's explore the Drama Triangle.

There are three roles in every triangle: victim, persecutor, and rescuer.

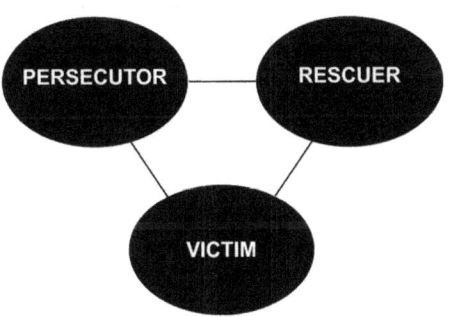

Figure 1. The Drama Triangle

Here's a quick outline of the three roles:

The Victim: *The victim feels powerless and at the mercy of circumstances and is unwilling to take responsibility for what has happened in their life.* The victim believes other people, things, or conditions are causing their troubles. In their mind, some unfair and undeserved threat, harm, or frustration has been inflicted upon them.

Victims are the star of their own story—the innocent "good guy"—and seek pity and sympathy for their plight. Through blaming a persecutor, they avoid responsibility for their situation.

The Persecutor: *The persecutor is the <u>perceived</u> cause of the victim's troubles.* The persecutor is seen as the transgressor—the "villain" in the drama story who has "done the victim wrong." Mostly, these are people but they can be institutions (such as companies or the government) or conditions (such as an illness, the traffic, or the weather).

The perception of persecution is *invented* in the mind of the victim based on the meaning they assign to an event. A perceived persecutor may not have ill intent or actually be doing anything harmful (such as insisting your child put their phone away and go to sleep).

A person who is truly *behaving* as a persecutor (by using force) often dominates and forces their will or conditions on another. Generally, persecutors don't see anything wrong with their actions and believe the victim deserved the consequences they are suffering. Through a twist of logic, persecutors often view

CHAPTER 4

themselves as victims, and blame the victim for their own abusive behaviors.

The Rescuer: *The rescuer intervenes on behalf of the victim in order to save them from their troubles.* They attempt to deliver the victim from harm or to make them feel better. Their form of helping is to soothe and reassure the victim or to "solve" the problem for them.

A rescuer can be a person; various forms of addiction including drugs, fame, and sex; or escapism such as daydreaming, exercise, reading, meditation, gaming, and social media. The rescuer can also be the *hoped for savior*, such as winning the lottery, a dream vacation, finding your soulmate, retirement, and such. *Noticing the times when you find yourself "hoping for a savior" can reveal situations where you are feeling victimized and participating in a drama story.*

> Drama isn't a cute and cuddly teddy bear; it is more like Chucky, the horror doll in the movies.

People with a habit of rescuing others need to feel important and to feel good about themselves. They want to see themselves as the "good guy" who has come to save the day. Ironically, the rescuer's intervention actually keeps the victim dependent, powerless, and stuck in their situation. Rescuers also exploit the victim for their own benefit, which is to feel better about themselves. In this light, rescuers can also be seen as persecutors.

In the drama story above (regarding having to work late), Terry is playing the role of the *victim*. His expectation to attend his daughter's recital was *thwarted*, so he reacts with anger and resentment. He claims innocence in this matter and believes he doesn't deserve this punishment. Terry is avoiding responsibility for being part of the team that didn't get the project done on time ... which caused the need for the overtime ... which caused him to miss his daughter's recital.

Terry perceives his boss as the *persecutor*. Renee is seen as the aggressor, the villain who is doing Terry wrong by making him miss his daughter's recital. Renee doesn't see it that way. He views himself as the good guy, doing what it takes to bring the project in on schedule.

Terry's teammates are playing the *rescuer* role by sympathizing with him. This helps justify Terry's belief he has been wronged and isn't responsible for missing his daughter's recital.

No matter which role you play in a drama, someone else is always a bad guy/villain. The victim sees the persecutor as the villain, as does the rescuer. The persecutor sees the victim as the bad guy and blames the victim for making them commit harmful behaviors. *The presence of a villain is a sure indication you are participating in a drama story.*

One important reason people engage in drama is to avoid feeling painful emotions. Terry feels terrible about missing his daughter's recital. He feels *guilty* for breaking his promise and *sad* about disappointing her. He probably isn't even aware of his deeper feelings of *shame* for failing to complete the project on time. Claiming the role of victim enables him to displace those emotions with much more comfortable ones: anger, resentment, and righteous indignation.

CHAPTER 4

As you just witnessed, *drama* can be a rescuer for avoiding pain. It transfers the focus from our shortcomings or culpability in a matter to how we have been wronged.

The Drama Not-So-Merry-Go-Round

To further explore the Drama Triangle, let's consider a more complex drama story Akeela shared with me early on in our coaching relationship.

After a long and grueling day, Akeela arrived home to find Tom sitting in the dark watching a sports channel with the sound off. Tom responded to her greeting with stony silence. He radiated barely contained fury; he was a ticking time bomb.

After putting her briefcase away, Akeela dutifully sat next to Tom and asked what was bothering him. Instantly, Tom exploded into a tirade. He catapulted to his feet and marched back and forth, raging about Sophie's *stupid* soccer coach and all of the *idiot* mistakes he was making. Tom threatened to "yank Sophie off that team so fast it would make the coach's head spin."

Tom's rage shocked Akeela. She sat there speechless, trying to control her panic as he continued.

During the soccer practice, Tom had walked over and offered the coach some well-meaning but unsolicited advice. The coach reacted by loudly telling Tom to leave the field and "remain on the sideline with all the other mothers." Tom seethed over that insult for the remainder of the practice.

When Tom's rant eventually wound down, Akeela was still in her own emotional reaction and so tried to rescue Tom. She sympathized with him, accusing the coach of being rude and thoughtless and similar criticisms. Tom ate it up.

Then she made the mistake of trying to fix it. Akeela asked Tom, "Did you talk to the soccer coach about your concerns?"

"Then Tom unloaded on me," she said. "He started cussing and calling me names and accused me of saying he was stupid, and I was always finding something wrong with everything he did."

Akeela left the house without another word. She spent the evening with a girlfriend who agreed that Tom had been a royal jerk. The friend urged Akeela to leave Tom and find a safe place to stay.

Although much more complex than the previous example, this is also a typical drama story. Only this time, the roles (victim, persecutor, and rescuer) *get swapped back and forth*, which is actually more commonplace than the simple drama described earlier.

> Drama is an attempt to get your needs met, only in a way that's neither constructive nor effective.

Let's start with what happened with Tom. This drama story began when Tom offered what he thought was helpful advice to the soccer coach. When the coach did not welcome Tom's advice and instead sent him to "stand with all the other mothers," Tom felt rejected, insulted, and humiliated. He took on the role of victim and made the coach

CHAPTER 4

out to be a persecutor. Tom did not take responsibility for butting in where no advice was asked for or wanted, or for getting upset when his advice was rejected.

When Tom told his story to Akeela, he wanted her to take his side and agree with him. At first, Akeela had sympathized with him. Tom started feeling justified in his outrage and felt gratitude toward Akeela. At this point, she was being a rescuer, which was what Tom wanted from her. Then, she asked about a possible solution, which would have been to talk to the coach about it afterwards.

Tom reacted strongly to Akeela's attempt to fix the situation. He took offense to her question and assumed the role of victim again, feeling persecuted by Akeela. He interpreted her question as an implication that he was stupid (another word for incompetent). You can imagine how this triggered his feelings of inadequacy from being unemployed. Then Tom switched to the persecutor role and verbally attacked Akeela, and she reacted by slipping into the victim role. (Are you keeping up with all this swapping back and forth of roles?)

Akeela then went looking for a rescuer to take her side against Tom and found one in her girlfriend. The two women then took on persecutor roles as they detailed Tom's faults.

Furthermore, let's assume Tom's unwelcome advice annoyed and possibly insulted the coach in this story. This caused the coach to become the victim to Tom's persecutor. Maybe he then counter-attacked as a persecutor to insult Tom, which catapulted Tom into his victim role. In a final touch of irony, Tom reacted to his *wife's* helpful advice the same way the coach did to *Tom's* helpful advice!

My head is spinning!

Now let's examine the consequences of all this drama.

- Tom's relationship with the coach is strained to the point where he is contemplating removing Sophie from the team (and you can image what drama would result from that).
- The coach probably thinks Tom is a meddler and a "coach wannabe" and wishes Tom wasn't around the team. And his negative opinion of Tom might filter down to how the coach treats Sophie.
- Tom and Akeela are mad at each other, and their already strained relationship has incurred even more damage.
- After Akeela "stormed out" (his words), Tom became afraid she would leave him, which deepened his already fragile sense of self-worth.
- Akeela's friend is alienated from Tom and afraid he might become physically violent.
- The friend's rescuing behavior deepened Akeela's hurt feelings toward Tom. It also increased the likelihood Akeela would seek rescuing in the future instead of staying and working it out with Tom.

This might have been riveting as a movie, but it was painful and very harmful in real life. That's the way drama is. It isn't a cute and cuddly teddy bear; it is more like Chucky, the horror doll in the movies.

I have ridden this Drama Not-So-Merry-Go-Round countless times in my own life. For instance, I have irritably

CHAPTER 4

snapped at my wife for questioning some decision I made. I felt insulted (victim) so I reacted with a biting comment (persecutor). She then became testy with me (persecutor). I felt victimized yet again because, after all, *she* instigated the whole affair with her inappropriate question. Then I realized I was responsible for my reaction, but because I was still emotionally triggered I went into rescuer mode to soothe her upset feelings. Thankfully, we calmed down and processed through the event in a healthy and loving way. But often, it's so easy to let the drama escalate.

Can you remember a time when the roles between victim, persecutor, and rescuer kept switching from one to another in your life?

Perfectly legitimate needs underlie every drama. Your drama is an attempt to get your needs met, only in a way that's neither constructive nor effective. Identifying these needs is key to being able to get your preferred outcomes. We will explore how to identify your core needs in Chapter 13, Max the Moment.

Since the motivations and mind-sets of each of the three roles are so similar, I will use the single term "reactor" to describe any and all of them.

The Trouble with Villains

Whether someone is a villain or not is *invented* by the perceiver. The victim invents a persecutor when they "villainize" someone as the bad guy in their story. And the persecutor does the same to the victim. The victim determines someone or something has treated them wrong, whether they have or haven't, and then characterizes them as the villain in their story.

An arresting officer is the villain to the lawbreaker. A loving parent becomes the villain to a willful child. A caring wife is the villain to a husband who wants to watch television rather than listen to her talk about her day. And the roles can easily reverse in each situation.

You may be wondering, "But what if they *really are* villains?"

Well, there are *relatively* few clear-cut situations in everyday life where someone has done something obviously "wrong" by social standards. For the majority of situations where you feel wronged, the other party also thinks you wronged them. Or it could be you are imposing your rules on someone else without their agreement. It all depends upon the perspective from which you see the situation. Then it becomes a "you said/they said" finger-pointing contest where nobody wins.

Let me be clear, people do commit offenses on other people. In many of those cases, apologies, restitution, or penalties may be warranted. But their behaviors do not make them a villain. Rather, they are people who made mistakes, acted out an emotional reaction in a harmful way, or gave in to a character weakness and harmed somebody. But everyone has done those things, including you and me. Are you a villain for your offenses?

Making someone into a villain can lead you to commit another wrong to try to make a right. You claim the right to become a persecutor to punish your persecutor. As the saying goes, it's an eye for an eye, right?

CHAPTER 4

Countless good guy/bad guy movies, books, and songs have made it abundantly clear: villains *deserve* to be punished. American Idol winner and country singer Carrie Underwood epitomizes this in her revenge song "Before He Cheats." The woman in the song strikes back at her man for cheating on her by trashing his vehicle. She slashed his seats, "keyed" the side of his car, smashed his headlights and punctured all of his tires. Too bad Underwood doesn't say what happened afterwards. Like how the woman went to jail, or how the man retaliated for her vandalism.

Force (violence) results when you conclude someone has hurt you and so deserves to be hurt in return. Once someone is villainized, the use of force is almost inevitable. People can justify almost anything once someone has been painted as a villain. Just consult the news headlines.

Force begets force, which perpetuates the cycle of drama, villains, and harm. Like some kind of demented whack-a-mole game, using force may appear to solve a problem, but it also creates more problems in its place. As Confucius said, "Before you embark on a journey of revenge, dig two graves." Below are some situations to illustrate this point:

- A baseball player is hit by a pitch. When the teams exchange places, the opposing pitcher retaliates and deliberately hits the first batter. The benches of the two teams empty in a free-for-all brawl.
- A boss continually bullies an employee at work. The employee goes home and abuses his wife and bullies his son. The son bullies a child in school

the next day and gets expelled. The wife numbs her misery through her addiction to pain pills.

- Frank seriously flirts with his friend Jamaal's girlfriend at a party. So, the jealous boyfriend flames Frank on Facebook. Frank, in a fit of anger, tells a lie about his buddy's infidelity to the girlfriend, who breaks up with Jamaal. The friends meet in a bar and are soon embroiled in a fistfight.

> *Force begets force, which perpetuates the cycle of drama, villains, and harm.*

Have you ever found yourself in a "force begets force" cycle of retaliation? How did it work out for you?

One of the key choices you can make to avoid drama is to refuse to villainize anyone. If there is no villain, then there is no need for force. You reframe your label of the other party through the lens of understanding and compassion. This is not to let the other person off the hook. Rather, it is to let *you* off the hook of emotional upset and the damaging cycle of force begetting force.

No matter what someone has done, you must realize the other party was driven by their emotional reactions in the same way yours drive you. You may not share their particular drama in this situation, but you have your own dramas.

We can develop compassion when we realize we are the "pot calling the kettle black." Getting upset and acting out is the human condition, something that we all share in common. Recognizing this can be a source of compassion that enables you to choose the creative path.

CHAPTER 4

The Antidote to Drama

Being a creator is the opposite of, and antidote to, being a reactor. A reactor *reacts with force*, whereas a creator *responds with power*.

The shift from being a reactor to a creator is what I call the Pivot to Power. The intent of this book is to offer you the practices, life skills, and mindsets that will enable you to make the Pivot to Power easily and skillfully.

Over the years, many people have developed positive alternatives to the Drama Triangle. In my opinion, none come close to my friend David Emerald's model called The Empowerment Dynamic™. David provides a masterful description in his highly recommended book *The Power of TED** and supports it with training you can learn about on his website, www.powerofted.com. This short and delightful story explains what David calls the Dreaded Drama Triangle (DDT)™ and The Empowerment Dynamic™ in much more detail than we will explore here.

The key role in The Empowerment Dynamic™ is the creator who takes on life's emotionally challenging situations in a positive and productive way. The creator says, *"I'm responsible for my life."* They tap into their personal power in order to choose their response to life's circumstances. They are *resourceful* in their responses, seeking positive outcomes for all parties involved.

At every step along the way, Tom, Akeela, the coach, and the girlfriend could have made different, more productive and more empowering choices. Let's replay the previous drama story and see what could have happened had anyone in the process exercised their power as a creator.

- Rather than interrupting the coach during the practice, Tom could have waited until later when the coach had the time to talk.
- Tom could have simply asked if the coach was open to hearing a suggestion. If not, he could have just dropped it.
- When the coach told Tom to go sit with the other mothers, Tom could have thought nothing of it. Or better yet, taken responsibility for his actions and apologized later for intruding on the coach's practice.
- Once Tom realized he was emotionally upset, he could have calmed himself down and let go of the drama story.
- Akeela could have realized how upset Tom was and withheld giving advice until a later time when he was in better shape emotionally and more open to discuss the matter.
- Akeela could have used empathic listening to validate Tom's experience without agreeing with it, thus enabling Tom to release his emotional charge.
- When Tom "unloaded on her," Akeela could have chosen to not take it personally, to recognize he was in terrible pain, and to excuse herself from the room (but not left the house). After he cooled down, she could have shared what she was feeling during his outburst and set a boundary with him about acceptable vs. unacceptable behaviors.

CHAPTER 4

- The friend could have listened to Akeela's pain with compassion and understanding, but then encouraged her to return home and address her concerns with Tom.
- The friend could also have chosen not to develop a negative story about Tom just because he acted poorly in this situation.

Any of those actions would have reduced or entirely eliminated the negative consequences created in the actual scenario. So why didn't someone take one of these positive actions?

Being positive and resourceful is easy when you aren't being challenged by difficult problems or unwelcome disruptions to your plans or desires. When you become emotionally triggered by a situation, it is hard to remain in creator mode, but that is exactly the moment when it is most needed.

My process for achieving the Pivot to Power is called Max the Moment. It is about *maximizing the moment of opportunity* when shifting into the creator mode to produce positive outcomes for whatever is upsetting you or others. I will explain that practice later, but we have a few other topics to cover before we get there.

Being a Creator is the opposite of, and antidote to, being a Reactor. A Reactor reacts with force, whereas a Creator responds with power.

One of the key questions to consider regarding emotional upsets is: why do we get triggered in the first place? The answer begins with how we create our reality.

CHAPTER 5

Choosing Your Reality

My wife and I happened on the show *Hit Record* with Joseph Gordon-Levitt while trolling Netflix for a movie to watch on a rainy weekend. The second episode of the series featured the theme "Fantasy," and I saw an immediate connection to what I'm sharing with you in this book. In one segment, Jacob Hirsch, Ph.D. from the University of Toronto shared this amazing observation:

> *"Most of us walk around with this notion in our heads that we see the world the way that it is. The reality that we have learned from neuroscience is that in fact, every perceptual experience that we have is an attempt by the brain to make sense out of the limited information that it is receiving."*

Dr. Anna Abraham, an associate professor of behavioral sciences, then noted:

> *"There's no such thing as an objective reality. Everything that you see through your eyes and your experience is in your mind."*

Dr. Hirsch went on to say:

"When you see something, and when you fantasize something, it's actually the same brain systems that are being activated. So, our perceptual experience, you could think of as a fantasy. <u>We are living a fantasy our entire lives</u>."

These ideas are certainly not new. What makes this remarkable is how mainstream these concepts have become, being featured in a pop culture venue such as this.

Back in the middle of the 20th century, author Anais Nin said the same thing worded this way: *"We see the world as 'we' are, not as 'it' is, because it is the 'I' behind the 'eye' that does the seeing."* And in the early 1800s, the legendary Henry David Thoreau said, *"The question is not what you look at, but what you see."* The esteemed scholar Alfred Korzybski put it this way; *"A person does what he does because he sees the world as he sees it."*

Therein lies the power to change your world ... your *thoughts* create your *reality*.

We are not troubled by things,
but by the opinions which we have of things.
— Epictetus, Greek Philosopher 55–135 AD

You can't change what happens to you and for you, but you can change how you *think* about what happens to you and for you. This world you experience is your fantasy, but is it a fantasy you are *choosing* to have or one that is *happening to you?*

CHAPTER 5

Are you being a reactor or a creator in relation to your own thoughts?

Your thoughts create your experience of, and response to, your world. If you want a different experience, you have to change your thoughts. One thought you may be having right now is "that's easier said than done."

Anyone who has made and failed at a New Year's resolution knows there is a big difference between wanting to make a change and being able to achieve it. There is a simple reason those desired changes don't last. The part of your brain that has the *desire to change* is *not* the part of the brain that *controls those behaviors.*

The subconscious *automatically* controls almost all of your thoughts, behaviors, and emotions based on what's happening in the present moment. The subconscious is like an autopilot that will run your life until you take charge. You will learn the tools for this later, but first you need to understand more about yourself.

> *Your thoughts create your reality, therein lies the power to change your world!*

Reality Is All in Your Head

Here's how your brain creates your unique view of "reality."

Everyone has a *mental map* they have developed over their lifetime. Sometimes it is called a "worldview" or a "paradigm." I refer to it as your "BIAS." BIAS is an acronym for beliefs, intentions, assumptions, and strategies.

Your mental BIAS serves both to explain the meaning of things and also to help you to cope with and thrive in the world. This is accomplished through the process of *perception*.

Every person in the world has an absolutely unique BIAS. Everyone experiences and understands the world differently than you do. There may be some—and sometimes a lot of—similarities, but there will *always* be differences. And those differences are often the source of conflict and misunderstanding.

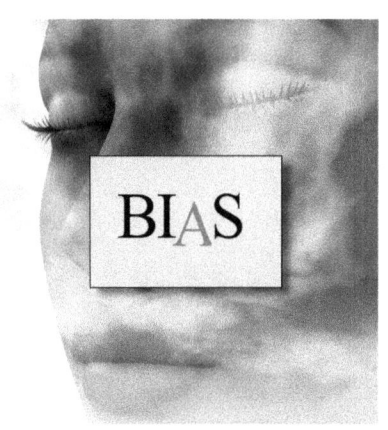

BELIEFS:
What we know, our experiences, what we hold as truths

INTENTIONS:
Values, goals, objectives and desired outcomes

ASSUMPTIONS:
Underpin the other three elements and hold them in place

STRATEGIES:
How we get things done, processes, approaches, plans

© 2016 Inner Mastery, Inc.

Figure 2. The BIAS Model

Everyone's BIAS is flawed (yes, yours too). Your BIAS is incomplete, inaccurate, and in many cases obsolete and ineffective. For instance, many of your beliefs, attitudes, expectations, and behaviors were formed before you were

CHAPTER 5

10 years old. How accurate and effective could they possibly be now?

Filtering and Distorting Reality

The diagram in Figure 3 illustrates how perception works. The process begins when something is seen, heard, or felt through your senses. This information is then *filtered* on two different levels before you act on it.

A "hardware filter" occurs because your physical senses are not able to take in all of the information available to you. This is a limitation of your physical body. For instance, dogs can hear frequencies humans can't. Those frequencies are available to us, but we can't perceive them. Also, there is a limit to how much information we can physically take in at one time. Imagine sitting at a sidewalk cafe. There may be dozens of conversations within earshot. But how many can you pay attention to at any one time?

Secondly, our BIAS serves as a "software filter." *We perceive what is important to us.* Our brain filters the incoming information and either prioritizes what is important to us or ignores and discards what is not.

> The subconscious is like an Autopilot that will run your life until you take charge.

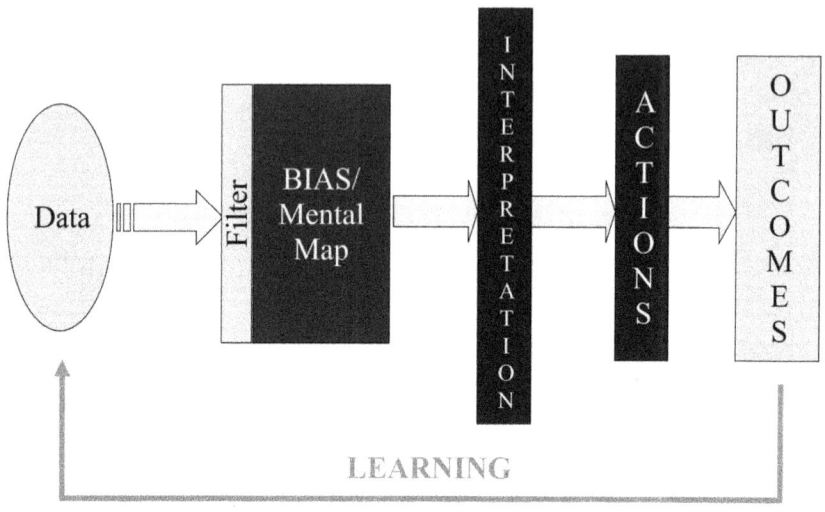

Figure 3. The BIAS Model of Perception

In my workshops, I ask participants to describe what is on the wall behind them. Despite having walked by the wall and seen it dozens of times, most can't recall the painting hanging there. However, everyone knows where to find the drinks and snacks. That's because the refreshments are more important to them than the painting. If you recall a time when you were thinking about buying a particular make and model of car, then you probably remember how you suddenly started to notice those cars everywhere. They were always there, but you didn't notice them before because they weren't important to you.

Another way our BIAS filters the information we perceive is *we see what we expect to see*. I've lost track of how many times I've been unable to find something in the kitchen only to have my wife walk over and locate it within a few seconds. Sometimes, it has been right on the

CHAPTER 5

counter in front of me. Because I didn't expect to see it on the counter, I *didn't* see it there ... even though it was right in front of me!

Finally, *our BIAS distorts what we perceive by changing it in various ways to fit what we already believe*—our current BIAS. This is called *confirmation bias*. Confirmation bias is one reason people find it difficult to understand someone else's point of view. Every time we look at the situation, our brain selects only the information that confirms our opinion about the matter and ignores or distorts anything that would contradict how we see it.

In the drama story described earlier, Tom interpreted the coach's comment in a negative way. He was predisposed to do so by his shame from being unemployed. He was primed and ready to be insulted. The coach's comments were interpreted through Tom's *filter of shame* and inevitably ended up making him feel even more ashamed.

Confirmation bias also contributes to keeping you caught up in drama stories, especially when you gather rescuers to agree with your BIAS. Getting multiple people to agree with your BIASed view does not make you more correct. Rather, it means many people are conspiring to participate in your fantasy with you.

> Every person in the world has an absolutely unique BIAS. Everyone experiences and understands the world differently than you do.

Our digital age has made confirmation bias an even bigger problem. People surround themselves on social media in "filter bubbles" with others who think the same way they do.

As a result, they successfully avoid those who might disagree with their perspective. This creates a sort of echo chamber where we hear our own opinions reflected back to us over and over, creating a deep certainty in our point of view as the truth. We firmly believe we are right and people with a different opinion are wrong. That leads to a polarized point of view. It's *us* vs. *them* thinking, which inevitably leads to conflict with *others* who disagree with us. We see this starkly in conversations about politics and other issues where people hold polar opposite perspectives.

Evidently, we are hardwired to seek out evidence that supports our BIAS. *Time* magazine (October 5, 2015, page 32) reported on an Emery University study:

> *Psychologist Drew Westin and his colleagues did brain scans on people who felt strongly about one or the other of two opposite positions. They discovered that when subjects rejected evidence that contradicted their position, their brain "lit up like addicts when they get a fix." Westin said "it appears as if partisans twirl the cognitive kaleidoscope until they get the conclusions they want, and then they get massively reinforced for it."*

In other words, we get a chemical high from being "right."

Stories Govern Our Lives

Through your BIAS, you construct a *story* about what is happening. Your story is an *interpretation* of the situation, the *meaning* it has for you. Certainly, there is nothing wrong with interpretations, especially since humans

CHAPTER 5

need to understand the meaning of a situation in order to function in the world.

Your interpretations/stories impact every aspect of your life. The meaning you assign to a situation triggers your emotions and your behaviors. "Positive" stories lead to pleasant emotions and productive behaviors. "Negative" stories lead to painful emotions and trigger Drama Triangle behaviors.

You cannot change your life for the better without taking responsibility for your emotions, and you cannot change your emotions without changing the stories that generate them.

Your BIAS contains countless stories you have accumulated over your lifetime. You have stories about

- love,
- relationships,
- trust and trustworthiness,
- money and wealth,
- health,
- physical appearance,
- social status,
- every person you know,
- what's possible and impossible,
- right and wrong, good and bad, or
- God and religion, and the list could go on and on.

Possibly the most impactful story you have is *who you are*—your identity. And it is just as much a fantasy within your control as all the other stories.

Your stories include *rules* you have for yourself, for other people, and many aspects of life. These rules arise from your BIAS: your beliefs, expectations, and strategies. Some of your biggest upsets occur when someone or something violates one of your rules. For instance, if it is important to you for people "to always be nice," you will become emotionally triggered if your loved one does something you interpret as "not nice."

You cannot change your life for the better without taking responsibility for your emotions, and you cannot change your emotions without changing the stories that generate them.

This upset occurs because you impose your rules on other people without their knowledge and agreement. This is called *"putting your map on someone,"* or *"mapping onto someone."*

Most of our rules are unspoken and have not been agreed to by the people upon whom we impose them. Our rules only erupt into view when they are broken and an upset ensues. Then we blame the other party for not knowing it was a rule and make them wrong if they disagree. We say things like, "I shouldn't have to tell you something like that, you should just know!" or, "*Everyone* knows you do (or don't do) that!"

Rules show up in the use of the words "should" and "should not." When you "should" on someone, you are making them wrong based on your rules. And "making people wrong" is part of the Drama Triangle—you are labeling the other party as the "bad guy," and usually you (or someone you are rescuing) are the "good guy."

CHAPTER 5

Big "T" vs. Little "t" Truth

Your stories, including your rules, create problems when you assume they are *absolutely true*—you aren't missing any information and your interpretation is totally accurate. Stories are an even bigger problem when they are treated as the *one and only Truth*.

Everyone has a *personal truth*—a small 't' truth, which is your limited and BIASed view of any situation. When you admit to yourself and others your understanding is valid yet limited, you create room for compromise and reaching a positive outcome.

The key is to qualify your statements by saying things like the following:

- In my opinion ...
- My understanding is ...
- What I'm thinking is ...
- The way I see it ...
- My expectation is ...
- My story about this is ...

Then the listener understands you aren't claiming you own the truth about a matter. There is room for an open-minded discussion and mutually beneficial outcomes.

On the other hand, if you assume your personal truth (your BIAS) is the *absolute Truth*—a big 'T' Truth—then conflict is inevitable. Someone has to be right and someone wrong. Someone has to win and someone has to lose.

You will jump into the Drama Triangle and start using force to get your way.

Be honest with yourself. How often do you have arguments with people, especially your loved ones, about who is right and who is wrong?

It is virtually impossible to know the whole truth about a matter. In the run-in with the coach, Tom's *story* is the coach told him to "go stand on the sideline with all the other mothers." But who knows what the coach *actually* said? This is merely what Tom *reported* to Akeela about the conversation. The coach might have simply asked him to go wait on the sideline. Since that is where the mothers were, Tom might have interpreted the coach was implying he was also a mother. Who knows?

Isn't it amazing how convincing people are when they tell us their drama stories?

That's because *people always slant the story to make themselves look good and someone else look bad*. So, of course, we get enrolled in their drama story. Reactors present their "facts" in ways that make it hard to see the situation from any other way. However, we never really know what *actually* happened when we hear a story second or third hand.

> Isn't it amazing how convincing people are when they tell us their drama stories? That's because people always slant the story to make themselves look good and someone else look bad.

Consider the extensive research revealing how eyewitness testimony in trials is notoriously unreliable. The Innocence Project reports an astounding 73 percent of the

CHAPTER 5

convictions overturned due to DNA evidence were based on eyewitness testimony. A full third of those involved two or more eyewitnesses!

A Stanford *Journal of Legal Studies* article notes the following research findings:

- The very act of making a memory introduces distortion.
- Using suggestive language in a question about an event can cause the eyewitness to remember the *suggestion* rather than the original *facts*.
- The act of telling a story to someone else shapes how you subsequently remember it, making it hard or impossible to recall your original understanding.
- People display even more confidence when reporting *misinformation* than they do when describing the original facts.

Memories are *reconstructed* rather than played back each time we recall them. The act of remembering, says eminent memory researcher and psychologist Elizabeth F. Loftus of the University of California, Irvine, is "more akin to putting puzzle pieces together than retrieving a video recording."

Every memory you have is a story you have constructed with some selective facts thrown in. You don't intentionally distort your memories; it is simply inevitable through the biology and psychology of the perception process itself.

Sit with that idea for a minute.

Since every memory is inaccurate to at least some degree, then it may be valuable to *automatically have some doubt about your recollection and understanding of a situation.* You might want to maintain at least a little doubt you are completely right about your understanding or someone else is wrong.

Fortunately, you can use the mechanics of memory and perception to your advantage. Since the meaning of a situation is *invented* through your BIAS, you can claim the power to change that interpretation to something more empowering!

Denise Michaels, a writer and friend, related a story illustrating this point: "Once I was driving across Las Vegas in rush hour traffic to attend a seminar. A friend travelled with me in the passenger seat. Four times during the drive, people cut over into the lane in front of me, narrowly missing my car. While she became angrier about each near miss, I thought, 'Well, they probably didn't see me in their blind spot.' No anger or upset. By the time we arrived, she was totally steamed, while I was calm and excited about the seminar."

> Since the meaning of a situation is invented through your BIAS, you can claim the power to change that interpretation to something more empowering!

You can change the story you tell yourself by changing what a situation *means* to you as Denise did in the story above. This is called a *reframe*. Later on, we will explore how to create a reframe when we discuss Max the Moment.

Your stories give rise to your actions, which create your outcomes. If you want different outcomes, you have

CHAPTER 5

to change your actions. And to change your actions you have to change your stories. You can't change your life unless you change your thinking … and that's an inside-out process.

Your stories are the *fantasies* you have about reality, which then *create* your reality.

You are making up the stories that are creating the life you have, and you have the power to choose *new* ones that will create the life you really want. Understanding this is key to your power to change your world.

You cannot avoid having an interpretation of a situation. The human mind just works that way. The choice you *do* have is whether to act out a drama story or an empowerment story.

Unfortunately, that is not always easy, due to the power emotional reactions exert over your thoughts and behaviors.

CHAPTER 6

Embracing Your Emotions

Being human means being emotional. So you would think, after all this time, we would be better at it by now!

During my public speaking events, I will often ask, "Raise your hand if you are emotional." I look out into the audience and see very few hands. Then I ask, "How many of you feel a lot of stress?" A majority of the attendees raise their hands. So then I explain that being stressed *is* being emotional, because stress is a messy mix of anxiety, fear, frustration, anger, irritation, and many other emotions.

> Being human means being emotional.

Why is it okay to admit being stressed but not emotional? When did having emotions become a source of shame?

Just consider the amount of energy people put into suppressing and avoiding their emotions. It's astounding really.

Our Struggle with Emotions

As I described earlier, my father was a hard man. His childhood was spent in abject poverty on an east Texas farm in a tough and unforgiving environment with a hard-as-nails father of his own (his destitute parents were forced to treat a near fatal burn on his leg with *turpentine*). I remember getting hurt and my father telling me to stop crying or he would "give me a good reason to cry" (which meant getting a whipping).

I wasn't allowed to cry. I wasn't allowed to be angry either because it was his private territory. I wasn't really allowed to have many emotions, including being too boisterously happy.

So, I learned how to quash my emotions pretty well and wear a "mask" of only positive emotions. And I have plenty of company in that. Practically everyone has emotions they are not comfortable experiencing or some they think are unacceptable to others and so they suppress them. Tom Lewis suffered terribly from the shame of his unemployment. But he wouldn't open up and talk about it with anyone, including his wife. His shame was too painful to admit publicly.

Frankly, we humans have some bewildering rules about expressing emotions.

Emotions are pretty much exiled from school, business, and social environments and also most homes, unless they are happy emotions. Actress and talk show host Ellen DeGeneres revealed in an interview that in her home growing up, "...the only feeling that was approved of was happiness—that was it." She also said, "I never saw

CHAPTER 6

anyone angry—so when I was 13 and my parents divorced it was a huge surprise to me because I thought everything was fine. It was very confusing."

Think about your own childhood home life, school experiences, work environments—how welcome has the expression of "negative" emotions been in your experience?

It seems anger, frustration, annoyance, irritation, and "strong" emotions are often okay if you are in a position of authority. Unless you are a woman, in which case those emotions quit being strong and simply qualify as "bitchy." My female clients tell me if a woman ever cries in a business setting, she will be labeled as emotional and lose much of her credibility. Akeela's boss used the terms "temperamental," "emotional," and "prickly" to portray the opinions some of Akeela's co-workers had of her. I don't recall him describing his male subordinates with any of those labels, despite ample evidence they fit just as readily.

It's almost never acceptable for a man to cry. While campaigning for the democratic nomination for president, Senator Edmund Muskie stepped up to a microphone to vehemently deny accusations of prejudice from what was later revealed to be a letter fabricated by political tricksters. The news reported he repeatedly broke down and cried during his speech. This simple and profoundly human act was viewed as a weakness and indirectly cost Muskie his candidacy. The event is now infamously referred to as "the crying speech." Muskie later claimed it was anger, not sadness, he was expressing, and those were melting snowflakes, not tears, on his cheeks.

Despite all the self-development I've invested in, I still struggle to cry in front of even my dearest and most trusted companion, my wife. These prohibitions of emotions can be very powerful and long-lasting.

Suppressing "Black Sheep" Emotions

Most people suppress certain "black sheep" emotions, including *shame, sadness, grief,* and *fear,* but these can be *any* emotion, depending on the individual. These types of emotions are often either too painful to endure, or too embarrassing to admit to anyone else. Referring back to Tom's run-in with the soccer coach, Tom felt *shame* when he was told to stand on the sideline, but what he showed publicly was *anger*.

Depending on your developmental experiences, any emotion has the potential to be on your "do not show this emotion under any circumstances" list. For instance, parents with anger issues often won't allow anyone else to show anger. As a result, their children may continue to suppress anger once they become adults, or maybe because they vowed to never be like their angry parent.

I recently read a social media post where a woman stated, "I never get angry. Ever!" Humans are wired to have emotions—*all* of the emotions. And each emotion has an important role in our lives. If you have an experience like this woman of never experiencing a particular emotion, you may be unconsciously suppressing it.

The suppression of emotions can lead to many different kinds of dysfunctional behavior. For instance, anger is

CHAPTER 6

crucial for holding boundaries. People who suppress their anger may display boundary issues, such as allowing people to take advantage of or abuse them.

Review this select list of emotions and identify the ones that you **do not** give yourself permission to feel and display to others:

anger, happiness, shame, contentment, sadness, frustration, fear, joy, grief, disappointment, resentment, guilt, jealousy, love, rage, regret/remorse, anxiety, embarrassment, pride, disgust, hope, desire, depression, passion, confidence

- Which of these are your personal black sheep emotions?
- Are there others not on this list you would add to the emotions you aren't willing to feel or show?
- What emotions do you substitute for your black sheep emotions?

When you suppress your negative emotions, you also limit your ability to feel the positive ones. When you reduce the lows, you also reduce the highs. Living a rich and fulfilling life will require you to welcome and experience *all* of your emotions. Although you may be subjected to more negative feelings, you will also feel greater joy, passion, and pleasure.

> When you suppress your negative emotions, you also limit your ability to feel the positive ones.

The full consequences from suppressing your emotions are described in the following chapter, and also in Chapter 9 during the discussion about the cost of stress.

Fortunately, there are things you can do to make it much easier for you to experience and process your painful emotions. We will explore these together in Part 2.

Thoughts vs. Emotions

People sometimes struggle to identify the emotions they are feeling and may confuse their thoughts with their emotions. Being able to identify your emotions is essential to processing them in a healthy manner.

Akeela invited me to dinner at her home with her and her husband, Tom. At one point, the conversation turned to a recent interview Tom had had with a prospective employer. He had received a rejection letter earlier that day and was still fuming about it.

After discussing it a bit, I asked him how he felt about the experience. He replied, "I feel that they made a poor decision."

I replied, "Well, that seems to be what you *think* about their decision making, but I am curious how you *feel* about this." He said, "Well I feel like I didn't get a fair chance at the job."

I explained again that his answer was a thought, and that I was looking to understand the emotion he was feeling. He snapped out a reply, "I'm sorry, but I don't know what you're talking about!" And then he excused himself from the table.

Like many people, Tom struggles to understand and express his emotions. (Read what happened next in Chapter 11 on Empathic Listening.)

CHAPTER 6

Focusing on your *thoughts* can keep you trapped in your drama story. Consider Tom's comments above:

- *"...they made a poor decision."* Instead of simply disagreeing with the decision, Tom disparaged their decision making. He took a persecutor role in this drama story.
- *"...I didn't get a fair chance at the job."* This is a victim story about being cheated.

Are those thoughts *more* or *less* likely to free Tom from his drama story and help him reclaim his power?

When you name the *emotions*, you are not engaging in your drama story. You are focusing on how the event affected you, which opens the door for you to process it in a healthy way. This a key part of the "Name It" step of the Max the Moment process we will discuss in Chapter 13.

Emotions are an internal experience. If what you are describing occurs *outside* of you, then that is much more likely a thought. For example, the statement "I feel disrespected" is what you *think* about how you were treated. That disrespect happened outside of you. In contrast, the statement "I feel angry and resentful" would capture the emotions that occurred internally when you were "disrespected."

All in all, we human beings are pretty uncomfortable with, and alienated from, our emotions. And we are experiencing serious repercussions in our own lives and throughout society.

Emotions Are Messengers

So let's start at the beginning.

You were born with a body fully equipped with a complete set of emotions. Your emotions are hard-wired into every aspect of your body and integrated into every part of your brain. Emotions are actually chemical cocktails that provide a particular quality of energy and spur a particular kind of behavior.

Emotion	Message	Energy
Anger	Something is threatening your boundaries! Protect yourself!!	Intense, aggressive
Fear	You are in danger <u>now</u>! Take action to protect yourself!!	Intense, defensive
Anxiety	A desired future outcome is at risk! Take action to ensure success!	Moderate, energizing
Impatience	Something isn't happening fast enough! Take action to move it along!	Moderate, aggressive
Frustration	After multiple attempts you still aren't getting your outcome. Try a different approach.	Moderate, aggressive
Sadness	You are hanging on to something that you are about to lose. Reflect on it then let it go.	Moderate, depressing
Grief	You have lost something important to you. Take the time to mourn the loss, then let it/them go.	Intense, depressing

Figure 4. Emotions as Messengers

Figure 4 shows a select list of emotions, their purpose, and the kind of energy with which they infuse your body.

I was explaining these emotions and the accompanying thoughts on this chart to a corporate group I was training when the vice president of finance asked me why we call these "negative" emotions. I acknowledged there are no "bad" or "negative" emotions. We impose these

CHAPTER 6

labels on emotions uncomfortable for us or for other people around us. They have a *negative effect* when acted out through a drama story and used to harm others. In their natural state, emotions are tremendous assets that support us and enrich our lives.

Emotions are designed to be resources to help us function effectively. You can think of emotions as *messengers*.

Your emotional messengers don't give up easily. If you get the message and act on it quickly, the emotions will go away by themselves. If you don't, they will keep coming back until you pay attention and do something about them.

In the movie *Serving Sara*, Matthew Perry portrays a legal process server tasked with chasing down an errant husband to serve him with divorce papers. Perry spends most of the movie chasing the man with many near misses until finally succeeding in the end. This is the way our emotions are. They keep returning until you get the message, act on the message, and then "dismiss" the emotion. Messengers don't hang around after delivering the message, but they won't stop until they do. If you will receive and act on the message from your emotions, their job is done and they will go away.

Natural vs. Reactive Emotions

Emotions are designed to pass quickly. If you get angry when someone cuts you off in traffic and nearly hits your car, that's normal. Staying angry, dwelling on it all day, or taking it out on other people is *not* how anger is supposed to work. Hanging onto emotions is toxic to you and to your relationships.

Emotions can be classified as *natural* or *reactive*.

Imagine waking up to a beautiful day and deciding to take the afternoon off from work and go for a walk in a rustic park. As you stroll down the dirt path, you enjoy the colorful flowers and their aromas, the caress of the gentle breeze and warm sun on your skin, and feel great about life. Then you round a bend in the trail and a giant venomous rattlesnake is sitting curled up in the middle of the trail, flicking its tongue and rattling furiously. What would happen to you?

Most people would have an immediate rush of fear. Fear is a messenger with a job to do. It warns us of immediate danger and delivers a jolt of energy, which enables you to flee or fight. In this case, let's say you immediately back away and then turn and run back to your car. Your heart is pounding and you are breathing rapidly, but now you are safe. In a few minutes, your heartbeat returns to normal and you have calmed down. So you decide not to risk the trail again and head home. Later that evening, you tell your harrowing tale and have some laughs with friends about your near miss.

That is how *natural* emotions function.

When on vacation in Hawaii, my son and I love to ride waves on boogie boards. So long as we stay on top of the wave, we have a lot of fun. But if the wave starts to break and we get caught in it, it slams us down and rolls us along the bottom. That experience is quite painful and also dangerous.

CHAPTER 6

In their natural state, emotions are like an ocean wave. They are designed to rise up, support you for a short period of time and then pass on, restoring you to a neutral emotional state.

However, if you get caught in the emotional wave (by clinging to your drama story), it will crash and tumble and drag you along the rocks, which is what happens with *reactive* emotions. The damage from emotions handled reactively is also quite painful and often dangerous to your health, relationships, and overall well-being.

Let's revisit your imaginary encounter with the rattlesnake.

Once you get back to the car, instead of calming down, let's pretend that you go into a drama story. You begin the drive home and start telling yourself a story that life isn't fair. You say to yourself, "The one time I take the afternoon off from work, there's a snake in the trail. Bad things always happen to me. And look at this stinking traffic now—I'm just in time for rush hour. Great! Just my rotten luck." You grouse and grumble to yourself all the way home and arrive in a foul mood. Instead of enjoying the company of friends that evening, you tell your drama story and pretty soon everyone is caught up in their own version of "ain't it awful." Your friends depart for home feeling upset and miserable.

> *Emotions are designed to pass quickly. Hanging onto emotions is toxic to you and to your relationships.*

The outcomes in this scenario are very different from the earlier description of the rattlesnake encounter. Getting hooked in a reactive emotion made your day miserable and then you infected your friends with the same poison.

A natural emotion is different from a reactive emotion in a couple of ways. First, there's no drama story involved in a natural emotion. And second, the emotion passes quickly and doesn't linger.

A reactive emotion can stay with you for hours, days, months, and sometimes years. Some people harbor their reactive emotions (their emotional wounding) over an entire *lifetime*. When emotions linger for hours or days they become a *mood* (I'm angry about something). Over a longer period of time, they become an *attitude* (I'm angry about everything); and over years, they become your *identity* (I am an angry person).

We are wired to have natural emotions. What transformed them into these destructive reactive emotions?

CHAPTER 7

The High Cost of Avoiding Emotional Pain

According to Bob Anderson and Bill Adams, co-authors of the superb book *Mastering Leadership*, 70 percent of adults function at what is called the *reactive* level of consciousness and in transition to the next level, while only 20 percent operate at the level of *creative* consciousness or higher. When things are going well, you must look closely to tell these two groups apart. But when there is a triggering event, the difference becomes unmistakable.

When upset, the reactive consciousness is predisposed to go into a drama story. Reactive people feel vulnerable and are afraid of being emotionally hurt or they are frustrated at the thought of not having their needs met. At this level of consciousness, your autopilot acts like it is a superhero whose job is to defend you from these threats. It leaps into action with pre-programmed reactions to attack, defend, or please in order to keep you safe and to get your outcomes.

Consider how Akeela reacted when she missed out on the big promotion she coveted. She became frustrated, angry, and resentful. In the weeks afterward, she became even more aggressive in defending her—and her team's—performance. Finally, the CEO had enough and sat her down and told her to tone it down.

At the higher level of adult evolution—the creative level of consciousness—people are mostly liberated from these fears. They have learned to separate their identities from their egos and so don't feel as vulnerable or see the same situations as threats. They are motivated by purpose and passion rather than external opinion. This enables them to operate at a very high level of functioning.

Through our coaching, Akeela learned to process her feelings about the missed promotion in a healthy manner. Also, she reframed the event to see it as a wake-up call. She embraced the coaching process and learned and grew tremendously. When the job opened up again a year later, she was offered the role without hesitation.

Since only 2 in 10 people function at creative consciousness or higher, you can expect the great majority of people to react emotionally when their ego is threatened. Which is another way of saying most people frequently get caught up in a drama story.

The Emotional Roller Coaster

The triggers for emotional reactions and drama are being *thwarted* in getting your needs met or being *threatened* with, or actually experiencing, *harm*.

CHAPTER 7

The ego, by its very nature, is self-centered. It works really hard to get what it wants (pleasure) and avoid what it doesn't want (pain). If something you desire is thwarted or denied you, the ego feels pain and reacts. If someone blames or otherwise finds fault in you, the ego reacts.

How do you feel when someone criticizes you, shames you, or makes you feel unloved and unwanted? You probably feel terrible. And how do you feel when someone compliments you, or when you are valued, admired, and loved by others? If you are like most people, you experience a positive rush and feel great about yourself.

> Up and down, up and down ... that's the typical emotional experience people have every day.

This emotional roller coaster is normal for most people. When your self-image is threatened or demeaned, you feel bad. When it's complimented and praised, you feel good. Life is a series of emotional ups and downs, coupled with extensive efforts to have more "ups" and avoid the "downs."

- Akeela felt great about herself when she made the shortlist in consideration for promotion to the VP of her department.
- Then she felt disappointed and angry when she wasn't selected.
- She felt great solving problems for her employees.
- Then she felt embarrassed and resentful when she was criticized for micromanaging.

Up and down, up and down … that's the typical emotional experience people have every day.

Fulfillment is a much more useful goal than happiness. Fulfillment comes from being filled with life—embracing the richness and complexity of your life in its totality.

For this reason, being *happy* is not a particularly useful measure or goal for the quality of your life. Happiness and unhappiness are *conditional* on things in your life going the way you want them to. When you like how things are, you are happy. When you don't like how things are, you are unhappy. Because life rarely lives up to our expectations, we can expect to be unhappy a lot.

Instead, you can choose to accept that life is the way it is—sometimes it goes the way we want and sometimes it doesn't. That's life. Fighting it is a losing proposition.

Fulfillment is probably a much more useful goal. Fulfillment comes from being *filled* with life—embracing the richness and complexity of your life in its totality.

If you want children, you are going to get a bundle of joy, but you will also get

- sleepless nights,
- visits to the emergency room,
- teenagers who scream "I hate you," and
- college students who forget you exist (at least for a while).

If you want a spouse, you may get romance and laughter, someone who believes in and supports you, and

CHAPTER 7

someone to wake up next to, take exciting trips with, and have a family with. You will also likely get someone who

- doesn't like you some of the time,
- has bad breath in the morning,
- is occasionally selfish, thoughtless, and uncaring,
- doesn't pick up after themselves, and
- won't keep their youthful figure as they age.

Fulfillment is embracing life on its terms, and saying "Yes!" to all of it. It means being equally okay with feeling happy and unhappy because you realize you don't get one without the other. The Inner Mastery practices in Part 2 will equip you to handle life's ups and downs much more effectively. However, the shift to a focus on fulfillment rather than happiness requires a conscious choice. I am confident that doing so will profoundly enrich your life!

The Root Cause of Reactions

You were born emotionally and psychologically whole and complete. Then as you grew older and interacted with your world, you began to get messages you weren't okay just being yourself. You received the message that something was wrong with you. You were only okay if you started being "good" (nice, pretty, neat, careful, happy, playful, positive, generous, etc.) and stopped being "bad" (mean, loud, dirty, irresponsible, unhappy, emotional, impolite, disrespectful, etc.).

As a result, many aspects of your ego were created in order to please other people—to gain their approval (pleasure) and avoid their displeasure (pain)—especially your parents, who were effectively "god-like" to you as an infant and young child. Your self-worth became dependent on other people. This process started with your parents, but later extended to your siblings, friends, acquaintances, and society in general.

When you attach your self-worth to forces outside of yourself, your sense of well-being becomes vulnerable. You become afraid of being emotionally hurt by other people's unflattering or critical opinions of you.

> People expend tremendous amounts of energy to protect their ego and to get positive reinforcement to ensure the answer to "Am I okay?" is always "Yes."

Young children are not psychologically equipped to process in a healthy way the negative messages they receive. The brain continues to develop throughout childhood, and critical thinking doesn't begin to develop until the age of 11 or later. Before then, children don't have the ability to evaluate and reject negative messages about themselves. Children accept these limiting messages as truth, and they become a part of the child's developing identity—their ego. These negative beliefs begin to operate from the level of their subconscious and give birth to the autopilot's job as superhero.

Children feel deeply ashamed to be so flawed and unworthy. Further, they believe that they are the only ones flawed like this—they are different from others—less than and undesirable. Have you ever felt that way? I certainly have and sometimes still do.

CHAPTER 7

This inadequacy is a profound pain most people go to great lengths to avoid feeling. We hide our shame and numb our pain. Limiting beliefs form your deep subconscious insecurities, such as:

- I'm not good enough.
- I'm not competent.
- I don't belong.
- I don't fit in.
- I'm unlovable.
- I am ugly.
- I'm stupid.
- I'm unwanted.
- I am worthless.

Whereas, we want to be seen as someone who is:

- good
- perfect
- likable
- popular
- successful
- attractive
- smart
- athletic
- talented
- important
- powerful
- wealthy

All the while, we fear deep in our hearts that we are none of those things.

The subconscious autopilot constantly guards for threats to the fragile ego. The autopilot continuously evaluates the questions "Am I okay?" and "Are we okay?" This results in anxiety and defensiveness. People expend tremendous amounts of energy to protect their ego and to get positive reinforcement to ensure the answer to "Am I okay?" is always "Yes."

Imagine your self-worth is a container filled with shining liquid. At birth, your container is full. You don't need anything else to feel good about yourself. You are enough just as you are. Your container has *integrity*, meaning it is functioning perfectly as it is designed, keeping all your shining self-worth intact.

Then, through your childhood you receive the message you are not enough—you are only okay if you do this or don't do that, become this and not that. These messages become limiting beliefs about yourself and the source of your insecurities. Each of these beliefs punches a hole in your container, causing your self-worth to leak out. As more and more holes are punched in the container, your self-worth drains out faster and faster.

You were born emotionally and psychologically whole and complete.

Losing this shining sense of self is painful. As your well-being drains out, you seek to refill your container through validation of your worth from people and things outside of yourself. You seek to be seen as valuable and worthwhile, as special, unique, and notable, and to avoid anything contradicting that image. This

CHAPTER 7

effort consumes your thoughts, energy, money—your life—and ultimately your health, serenity, and fulfillment.

Due to the holes in your container, your attempts to fill it up are fruitless. No matter how much validation you put in, it will never be enough. And when the pain of your inadequacy becomes too much, you seek ways to numb it.

People don't want to feel pain. They especially don't want to feel emotional pain, and the "black sheep" emotions described earlier—shame, fear, sadness, and grief—are the most painful of the lot.

Emotional insecurity is pervasive in society and that adds up to a lot of pain—and a lot of money and effort spent avoiding or numbing that pain. We go about this in many ways, and in particular through drama, addictions, and behavioral compulsions.

Drama Distracts Us from Pain

Drama and reactionary behaviors are ways of avoiding or displacing the pain of your insecurities. Instead of looking inward for the source of your pain, you might choose to redirect your attention elsewhere, to something less painful. You engage in the Drama Triangle. You may

- blame others,
- attack someone's character,
- make people feel stupid,
- overpower others through force or authority,
- confuse the issue,

- nitpick,
- rationalize,
- criticize,
- shut down emotionally,
- act hurt, or
- become a peacemaker and "go-along to get-along," and any other of hundreds of similar reactions.

Even if you ultimately accept responsibility, your reaction still achieved your goal, which was to avoid looking inside yourself and facing your painful feelings.

In contrast, when you turn *toward* your emotions and process them in a healthy way, your drama story loses most or all of its power over you. Releasing your emotions makes it much easier to find a positive resolution to your situation. In addition, draining those emotions will be very healing for you. You are supporting your body to process these as natural emotions instead of reactive ones.

Numbing Through Addictions

Addictions are common ways people numb themselves from their painful emotions. Addictions are defined as activities you can't stop yourself from doing.

These can include food, sex, cigarettes, alcohol, drugs (including abuse of prescriptions), and gambling. Each of these can take a huge toll on a person's health and overall well-being, not to mention the enormous impact on their families, communities, and society in general.

CHAPTER 7

Research indicates 40 million people are addicted to cigarettes, and a third of the population of the US — that's 80,000,000 people—are "risky" substance users. One in ten people over the age of twelve— 23.5 million Americans—suffer from alcohol abuse, dependency, or binge drinking. That's roughly the population of the state of Texas. An astounding 52 million people have used prescription drugs for non-medical reasons. Nearly 12 million people are addicted to sex, and from 5–7 percent of the US population are addicted to gambling.

Enough already! These are mind-boggling and heartbreaking numbers. I think you and I both have a good idea about the staggering financial and social cost these addictions inflict, so I will not belabor them here. Odds are that one way or the other you have personally experienced the costs of addiction.

Numbing Through Compulsive Behaviors

Compulsive behavior is defined as performing an act persistently and repetitively without it necessarily leading to an actual reward or pleasure. These behaviors serve to help avoid or numb emotional pain. Examples of compulsions can include busyness, shopping, hoarding, workaholism, social media, gaming, exercising, religiosity, and greed for wealth, beauty, power, and celebrity status.

In our society, *behavioral compulsions* are often viewed with tolerance and some are even celebrated as badges of honor. Perhaps one of the most pervasive of these compulsive behaviors is "busyness." Some of the most common refrains I hear are "I am insanely busy," "There's just not enough time to do everything I need to do," "It's another crazy-busy week." Busyness, and the resulting stress, seems like an epidemic.

Busyness serves an important purpose for the ego. If you stay busy enough, you never slow down long enough to feel the full brunt of the pain built up inside. Often, for some people, a strong feeling of anxiety arises from not having something to do and being stuck with just their thoughts.

A study by the University of Virginia revealed a startling finding. Given the choice between sitting quietly and thinking for 6 to 15 minutes in an empty room or giving themselves a painful electric shock, 67 percent of men and 25 percent of women chose the electric shock to boredom! Jonathan Schooler, a psychology professor at UC Santa Barbara who studies consciousness noted, "I found it quite surprising and a bit disheartening that people seem to be so uncomfortable when left to their own devices; that they can be so bored that even being shocked seemed more entertaining."

> *The key to healing is facing the painful feelings of inadequacy and challenging the false beliefs that convinced you something is wrong with you.*

The key to healing is facing the painful feelings of inadequacy and challenging the false beliefs that convinced you something is wrong with you. When you face the pain and process it effectively, you will be better equipped to challenge and dismiss the false assumptions underpinning your insecurities. You will permanently plug the holes in

CHAPTER 7

your container of self-worth, releasing you from the compulsion to constantly refill it.

The development of Inner Mastery is a journey to free yourself from the chains of your personal dramas and the suffering they inflict.

CHAPTER 8

The Secret for Reprogramming Your Autopilot

What percentage of your life do you believe is being run by your subconscious and how much of what you do is being chosen consciously?

My clients typically say the subconscious accounts for about 50–75 percent of their thoughts and behavior. But their estimate is way too low. The actual amount is more like 95 to 98 percent!

Yeah, I was shocked too. However, when you consider how many things we do without thinking about it over the course of a day, it's not so hard to believe. You don't have to think about how to tie your shoes, use a faucet, drive your car, and most other routine activities in life, you just do them automatically. Your subconscious handles those activities for you. And thank goodness it does! How overwhelming would it be if we had to think about every single thing we do all day long?

> The subconscious accounts for 95-98% of your thoughts and behaviors.

The *conscious* part of you, the "executive function," resides behind your forehead in the neocortex portion of your brain. This part of your mind can observe, engage, and change the subconscious. The name we will use for this part of your mind is the *pilot*. Everything else is the *subconscious*, which we have been referring to as the *autopilot*.

The "Parts" of Your Autopilot

The subconscious is made up of many different parts (you could also call these "voices"). These parts are your learned habits, or more specifically, your learned *patterns of behavior*. Examples of your patterns of behavior include the part of you that

- gets angry when someone makes fun of you,
- becomes frustrated when things don't go your way,
- feels good when people praise you, or
- does nice things for people you love.

Do you recognize any of these as parts of your own autopilot?

Almost everyone has experienced talking to themselves. Often it seems multiple voices in our heads argue a point at the same time. The Pixar/Disney movie *Inside Out* richly illustrates the automatic parts of our subconscious.

Each person in the movie is shown to have five emotions in their minds, described as "inside voices." These parts control or affect the thoughts, emotions, and

CHAPTER 8

behaviors each person experiences for every situation. A different part, or emotion, runs the "control panel" for each of the main characters. The little girl Riley's lead emotion is "Joy," the mother's is "Sadness," and the father's is "Anger." Of course, the movie is a greatly simplified version of what really happens in our minds, but it does illustrate the concept quite well.

One key omission from the movie—and it's a BIG one—is the absence of a character to represent the pilot, which is the adult voice in your head. The pilot is immensely important because it enables you to regulate and moderate your emotions—to choose how you will respond to any given situation rather than just reacting.

Each of these "voices" is a part of your subconscious. Parts are like versions of you who live in the subconscious—they *include* emotions but are more than just emotions.

Subconscious parts are the result of your learning process. When you encounter a *new* need or challenging situation in your life, you try out several methods for getting what you want. When something works, you try it again. If it keeps working, you refine it through repeated practice and then memorize it as a *pattern of behavior*. These patterns become the parts of your subconscious.

"Triggers" Are Programmed in Your Autopilot

Reactions require a triggering event which signals the subconscious to do something. That *trigger* then activates a combination of memorized *thoughts* about what this event or situation means, *emotions* based on those thoughts, and *actions* you should take to get your desired outcome. This usually happens so fast you don't even realize it's occurring.

The autopilot doesn't think, it just reacts to a trigger and rockets into action to do what it is programmed to do. You might have heard the expression "having your buttons punched," which means something happened that caused you to have an emotional reaction. These "buttons" are "triggers."

A trigger is a stimulus that normally comes from *outside* of you, but we can also trigger ourselves. A trigger can be anything, for example:

- a sound (like a loud bang)
- an expression on someone's face (like rolling their eyes at you)
- something that is said to you (like an insult or sarcastic comment)
- a behavior (like someone leaving the lid up on the toilet)
- critical self-talk (like calling yourself an idiot for making a mistake)
- something that *didn't* happen (like not getting a card on your birthday)
- something that doesn't have anything to do with you (like movie stars getting divorced)

You may or may not have had anything to do with causing the triggering event.

CHAPTER 8

In contrast, *your reaction <u>always</u> comes from within you*. You are 100 percent responsible for your drama stories, emotional reactions, and reactive behaviors. The triggering event becomes data that you interpret through your BIAS. If you conclude that you are being thwarted, threatened, or hurt, then you will generate a drama story. Your drama story then gives rise to your emotional reactions and your behaviors.

The idea that *you*—and not your villain—are responsible for your reactions can be a bitter pill to swallow at first. Yet accepting this truth will open the door for you to create the life you want. It's that important. Until you accept responsibility for your drama stories and reactions, you will remain a puppet to your autopilot and a victim of the circumstances constantly swirling around you.

> Your reaction always comes from within you. You are 100 percent responsible for your drama stories, emotional reactions, and reactive behaviors.

Triggers don't have to generate negative reactions—they can just as easily be used to create positive responses. In fact, you can intentionally create your own triggers to accomplish exactly that. You will learn how to take advantage of this capability in Part 2 when we explore creating "power phrases."

A power phrase is a trigger that generates positive thoughts, emotions, and behaviors and leads to constructive outcomes. You probably already use power phrases in your positive self-talk, if you've ever said or thought:

- Don't sweat the small stuff.
- This too will pass.

- Don't take it personally.
- It is what it is, accept it and move on.
- That's their pain speaking.
- What would Jesus do?
- Don't take their monkey.

As you read along, write down or highlight any phrases that catch your eye that you might want to adopt as a power phrase for yourself.

Reprogramming Your Autopilot

The subconscious is quite a lot like a computer. You can "reprogram" your subconscious parts to be the way you want them to be once you learn the programming language. You created these parts in the first place and you can recreate them to be something else. The strategies in this book take advantage of *neuroplasticity*, which is the ability to reprogram your brain to think and behave differently.

Symbols in the form of *metaphors* are the programming language of the subconscious.

Your digital devices (smart phone, tablet, computer) all have a graphical user interface (GUI). This GUI simplifies the complexity of a computer's bits and bytes (1s and 0s) and enables you to interact with it through simple and familiar metaphors: click a button to open an app, slide a lever to increase the sound volume. There actually is no button or lever, just photons on a screen, which the software translates into machine code. But

CHAPTER 8

that doesn't matter to you, because it works. Thanks to those metaphors, you don't need to know how to write computer code.

Metaphors are also the GUI for the subconscious mind. I don't know how to directly rewire the neurological pathways to make my brain think and function differently. However, if I perform a visualization exercise, my subconscious will do the programming for me because it *does* know how to make those changes.

So, your subconscious mind works basically the way your computer screen works, through user-friendly metaphors.

Visualizations are how we construct metaphors to achieve our desired outcomes. The brain "programs" meaning based on the only thing it knows, which are the five senses: sight, sound, sensations, taste, and smell. When you create a rich visualization using those senses, you can have a powerful effect on changing your subconscious programming.

Each of the senses are processed in different sections of the brain. Vision is processed by the occipital lobe in the back of the brain, sound in the temporal lobes above the ears, and sensations in the parietal lobe in the center of the brain.

The more senses you involve in your visualization, the greater percentage of

> *Until you accept responsibility for your drama stories and reactions, you will remain a puppet to your autopilot and a victim of the circumstances constantly swirling around you.*

the brain is involved in making the change. A *rich visualization* includes all three primary senses: pictures, sounds, and sensations. You will be using visualizations in many of the techniques shared in this book to achieve profound shifts in how you think, feel, and behave.

Visualizing something with full senses (seeing, hearing, feeling) engages the same parts of the brain as directly sensing the outside world. Your subconscious does not know the difference. (Recall our earlier conversation about the same parts of the brain processing both external senses and our internal fantasies.) Athletes have used this phenomenon for decades to visualize their performance in advance of the event, resulting in dramatic improvements.

You too can take advantage of the power of visualization to change your life through the many practices described in Part 2.

PART 2

Create a Great Life

CHAPTER 9

Mindfulness — Laying the Foundation for Power

Mindfulness is the ability to maintain a state of inner calm and focused awareness.

Practicing mindfulness on a consistent basis enables you to remain centered and powerful in the face of your daily challenges. It provides an inoculation against stressors, which increases your resilience and ability to remain composed. Mindfulness helps ward off many minor emotional triggers that would have otherwise induced you to react.

Mindfulness has many benefits, including:

- diminished stress
- reduced depression
- enhanced memory
- increased focus
- less emotional reactivity (drama)

- greater self-awareness
- improved relationships
- better health

Not a bad return on your investment of just a few minutes each day!

We will start our discussion of mindfulness with stress management techniques and then explore ways to clear your mental clutter and stay mentally quiet and focused.

The True Source of Stress

Stress is one of the biggest contributors to people's emotional reactions.

Practicing mindfulness on a consistent basis enables you to remain centered and powerful in the face of your daily challenges.

Imagine this scenario. You arrive home from work on a Friday evening and within minutes of walking in the door, your spouse says to you, "We need to talk about our daughter; she cheated on a test and got expelled from high school for three days!" Your day has been brutal, and you have already endured a long and stressful week. You had back-to-back meetings all day and didn't even stop for lunch. Your project suffered a serious setback when a vendor notified you they will miss the deadline for an essential part of your design. A wreck snarled rush hour traffic, and your nerves are completely shot.

CHAPTER 9

Now, what kind of shape are you in to deal effectively with the crisis with your daughter?

This is the story Akeela shared with me in one of our meetings. She was still upset about the event days later because she felt she had handled it poorly. Tom was angry when Akeela walked into the house, and his being upset along with her high level of stress led her to verbally unload on Sophie about her behavior. Her daughter then ran from the room crying and locked herself in her bedroom.

The purpose of this scenario is to illustrate the consequences of stress on your ability to be powerful.

Almost anyone as stressed as Akeela would have behaved poorly in this situation. If she had been able to respond powerfully, Akeela might have sat down with Sophie and calmly asked her to explain what had happened at school. Based on the facts, Akeela could have worked out an appropriate resolution and action plan. (As it turns out, another student had copied Sophie's test answers without her knowing it, but both were expelled anyway.)

When you are relaxed, unstressed, and feeling good, you can access your power pretty easily. Then you can respond effectively when a challenging situation arises. That's the value of mindfulness.

Many people have the mistaken notion that stress comes from outside of us and happens to us, like catching a cold.

Stress is actually the *emotional response we create internally* in reaction to *external pressures*. Events outside of us may be *stressors* that exert pressure on us, but only we can create a stress response to that pressure.

The late, great Dr. Wayne Dyer used the metaphor of an orange to explain this. Squeeze an orange hard enough and it will burst and juice will squirt out. The hand is applying pressure, but the juice comes from within the orange.

When life "squeezes" you, what "juice" (emotions and behaviors) comes out?

Two primary sources of stress are physical and emotional pain. Physical pain and discomfort introduce stress on your body and mind. If you have back pain, you will have some stress regardless of what else is happening in your life. Other physical factors that have a big impact on stress include the quality of your diet, whether you are getting enough exercise, and the amount of restful sleep you are getting each night.

Emotional pain comes from the thoughts you are having about your life or a specific situation. Examples are worrying about an important presentation you have to make, being angry and resentful about your performance rating in a recent review, and feeling sad about yelling at your children.

> *Emotional pain comes from the thoughts you are having about your life or a specific situation.*

For most people, emotions are the greatest contributor to their feelings of stress, which is actually good news! *You can change your thoughts and emotions and dramatically reduce or even eliminate your feelings of stress, regardless of whether anything else changes in your external environment.*

CHAPTER 9

Stress Increases Reactive Behaviors

Most people, when stressed, are much more likely to resort to negative and forceful behaviors. Dr. Sherry Buffington, developer of the CORE Multidimensional Awareness Profile (CORE MAP®) personality assessment tool, has included in her model a profile of a person's *stress coping style*. In other words, the behaviors people engage in as they become increasingly stressed.

CORE stands for the four personality types in the model: Commander, Organizer, Relater, and Entertainer. For each of the personality types, there are positive qualities they tend to display when at their best. Each type also has predictable negative qualities they demonstrate under stress. See Figure 5.

As stress escalates, people become increasingly less effective—less resourceful—and more negative. People first move into a moderate expression of these negative qualities. If stress continues to increase, they ultimately express the most negative qualities.

Take a moment to review the list of these behaviors below. Which qualities do you recognize in yourself? In your loved ones and co-workers?

Commander	Entertainer
Under Stress Becomes: • Impatient, Blunt, Dominating • Intimidating, Pushy, • Louder, Demanding • Insensitive, Belligerent • A User/Abuser – Do it my way! • Overpowering, Humiliating	*Under Stress Becomes:* • Interruptive, Pushy, Argumentative • Unfocused, Hard to follow • Close one moment, Distant the next • Impatient, Intrusive, Obnoxious • Self-centered, Superficial • Pay attention to ME! type
Organizer	**Relater**
Under Stress Becomes: • Passive-aggressive • Dwells on details • Withdrawn, Cold • Self-righteous • Stubborn, Narrow-Minded • Shames or Embarrasses others • Silent or Sarcastic	*Under Stress Becomes:* • Passive, Submissive • Struggles to set priorities • Self-sacrificing, Blame-taking • Obstinate, Unable to decide/act • Silent or Tearful • Withdrawn, Hurt, Hypersensitive • Manipulative with Guilt or Pity

Figure 5. The COREMAP Types Under Stress

This concept was a revelation for me. When people exhibit these negative characteristics, they aren't *character flaws*, they are the *predictable behaviors of a personality type under stress*. These negative behaviors aren't a question of *character*, but of *competence*. While character is considered to be something fairly permanent, skills can be learned!

And the even bigger insight is this: *when you increase your ability to handle stress and are able to stay calm and relaxed, you naturally demonstrate your best qualities.*

CHAPTER 9

That's a big deal because stress is so pervasive in modern society. A recent American Psychological Association study reported that an astounding 41 percent of Americans report *chronic* work-related stress. And that was nearly 15 percent higher than just the year before!

The Sky-High Cost of Stress

There's also the toll on health to consider. The World Health Organization estimates that stress costs American businesses alone *$300 billion per year!* That's not so hard to imagine given the results of a study by a global HR development company. The study indicated stress as the most common cause of long-term sickness and absence for employees.

Research has shown stress to be a major contributor to practically every chronic illness plaguing our society today:

- Heart disease and heart attacks
- High blood pressure and strokes
- Obesity
- Cancer and increased rate of tumor growth
- Fertility and libido problems
- Reduced bone density
- Dementia and Alzheimer's
- Accelerated aging
- Virtually all auto-immune illnesses

- Type 2 diabetes
- Fibromyalgia
- Allergies and asthma
- Intestinal diseases (Crohn's, Irritable Bowel Syndrome, etc.)
- Rheumatoid arthritis
- Lupus

Yikes! We pay an incredibly high price for stress. But there's reason to hope: reducing stress throughout society has the potential to reduce negative behaviors and improve health on a widespread scale!

You have the power to manage your emotional reactions to stress. And the positive outcomes are well worth the small amount of effort required.

Assessing Your Stress Level

How stressed would you say you are on a typical workday? Use a 10 point scale where "1" is very low stress, like when you have been relaxing on vacation for a week, and "10" would be maximum stress.

So on that scale of 1 to 10:

- What number would you say is your average?
- What number do you hit when your stress peaks?
- What number do you hit when you are your most relaxed?

CHAPTER 9

Write those three numbers down—your average, high, and low.

According to the American Psychology Association, a healthy average stress level is 3.7 on a 10-point scale. For ease of use, let's round that to an even 4. How does your stress level compare? Almost all of my clients report an average of 6–7 and a peak of 9–10. That's high!

Stress levels correlate to brain frequencies. Take a moment to review the frequencies shown in Figure 6.

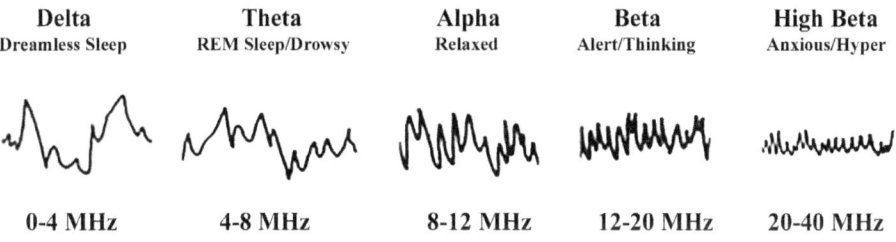

Figure 6. Ranges of Brain Frequencies

Frequencies in the High Beta range are considered to match up with *chronic stress*. When you convert the 40 MHz scale to a 10-point scale, it means anything above a 5 on our 10-point scale is considered to be chronic stress.

Healthy levels of stress average 4 and rarely exceed a 5. Figure 7 converts our 10-point scale to a color chart of Green (1–4), Yellow (5–6), and Red (7–10) levels of stress.

	Physical	Mental	Emotional
1-4	Physically relaxed and calm	Mentally relaxed and focused	Emotionally positive, light-hearted and upbeat
5-6	Moderately tense and tired or amped up	Mind is <u>somewhat</u> tense and distracted	Moderately anxious, worried, or emotionally upset
7-10	Very tense and tired or amped up	Mind is racing and very difficult to stay focused	Very anxious, worried, upset and easily "triggered"

Figure 7. Levels of Stress

Tracking Your Stress

Using the chart above as a guide, I recommend you track your stress levels for a week, including the weekend. This will give you a more accurate gauge of your stress and will also give you insights into what triggers your stress.

1. Track your stress level each day for a week and write it down on a piece of paper.

CHAPTER 9

2. Use the Green, Yellow, Red categories shown above, and record your scores at least four times per day: morning, lunch, late afternoon, evening. Recording them every hour is even better.
3. Use the reminder function on your phone or something similar to alert you to check your stress level.
4. When the chart is complete, evaluate it to better understand your stress patterns throughout the week. What insights does it give you?

4 Steps to Manage Your Stress

All of the techniques for Inner Mastery we introduce throughout the book will help you reduce your emotional reactions and your overall stress. In this section, I want to focus on four simple, fast, and easy techniques for getting control of your stress.

1. Master Your Breathing

When stressed, you breathe shallowly. You breathe high in the chest in small breaths like you are panting. Since the 4- to 6-inch length of the trachea between your mouth and the entry into the lungs is "dead air," shallow breathing draws very little fresh air into the lungs. The resulting physical distress increases your overall stress reaction.

The solution is to breathe deeply and slowly. Flooding the brain with oxygen in this way changes your brain chemistry immediately, helping to relax your body and mind.

"Belly breathing" (also called abdominal or diaphragmatic breathing) is our natural way of breathing. Watch a baby breathe when she sleeps and you will see her belly rising and falling. Your goal is to deliberately belly breathe when you notice yourself starting to react or become stressed. I recommend that you eventually adopt abdominal breathing as your normal everyday style.

This breathing practice uses an 8-4-8 cycle: breathe in for a count of 8—hold for a count of 4—breathe out for a count of 8. There are many other breathing practices that work just as well. Dr. Andrew Weil advocates an ancient yogic cycle of 4-7-8: breathe in for 4—hold for 7—breathe out for 8. I recommend you find a breathing cycle that works best for you and use it in your breathing practice.

<u>For your first time only:</u>

    a. To get used to belly breathing, lie face up on the floor. Place your hands over your navel and gently blow out all of your breath through your mouth.

    b. Breathe in slowly and deeply and try to make your hands on your belly rise. Once your belly is full, continue to fill your lungs and feel your chest expand. Use a count of 8 to complete your in-breath.

    c. Hold your breath for a count of 4.

    d. Exhale gently and naturally through your mouth for a count of 8 until all of the air is out of your lungs. Feel your hands on your navel drop with your out-breath.

CHAPTER 9

<u>Thereafter</u>

    e. Repeat the breathing pattern of 8-4-8 four times. After some experience with this method, you can work your way up to a max of 8 cycles.

    f. Deliberately relax your muscles with each out-breath. Feel the tension releasing and imagine it flowing down and out of you like water.

    g. Keep your attention on your breathing. Follow the breath through the nostrils into your lungs and then back out again. This will help you to increase your concentration and focus.

    h. Notice how you feel after using this style of breathing. Through this technique alone, you will be much more relaxed and feel quite a bit calmer than before.

Pick a quiet time when you know you'll be uninterrupted and can focus on your breathing. At the office, you might not be able to lie down on the floor, but you may be able to close your office door, relax in your chair and choose to filter out the noise or sound from down the hall.

After you get used to this style of breathing, you can use this exercise any time you start to feel stressed. You can even perform this exercise in the middle of a meeting without anyone noticing. (Except, of course, for the part about lying on the floor.)

I recommend you start and end your day with this deep breathing practice. You will energize your body to start your day, and flush the toxins from your brain at the end of the day so you can sleep better.

2. Center into Your Body

Mental fatigue is one of the causes of stress. This comes from "being in your head" too much (thinking too much). When you think too much, you lose touch with your body. Your brain moves into the high-beta frequencies related to chronic stress. These frequencies exhaust the brain, whereas frequencies at alpha and lower (a 4 or lower on the 10-point scale) are restful and rejuvenating for the brain.

When you put your awareness on the sensations in your body (without analyzing those feelings!), simply sensing them, the brain moves into an alpha frequency and your mind and body relax.

Couple this exercise with belly breathing to enhance the positive benefits of both.

a. Pay attention to the feelings inside your body. Starting with the top of your head, slowly scan downward. Simply notice what sensations you feel in the various parts of your body. Slowly continue down your body to the bottoms of your feet.

b. If you notice tense areas, you can clench and relax any tight muscles to help release the tension. (You can also use the "Drain the Pain" technique you will read about in a later section to amplify the benefits.)

c. Shift your awareness to your external senses. Start by noticing what you feel on your skin. What temperature do you feel? Do you feel any air moving against your skin? What textures can you feel from your chair, your clothes, your desk? What does your body feel like pressing into the chair? Your feet pressing into the floor?

d. Now close your eyes and focus on the sounds around you. Simply become aware of the sounds without analyzing them. Continue this for a minute or more.

e. Now open your eyes and notice what you see. What colors do you observe? What patterns are the ceiling lights or sunlight making around you? Try to see the shapes around you as circles, triangles, rectangles, and lines instead of the things themselves. See the objects around you as if you had no names for them.

f. Notice what has shifted for you after this practice. Most people feel not only calmer but more aware, more mindful.

Repeat this exercise several times per day, and anytime you are feeling mentally fatigued.

3. Practice Gratitude

In her book *Living in Gratitude: A Journey That Will Change Your Life*, Angeles Arrien defines gratitude as "the acknowledgement of the positive things that come our way that we did not actively work toward or ask for." It is appreciation for the unearned gifts we receive through the course of our day.

Practicing gratitude can improve your health, happiness, well-being, and your relationships. Feelings of gratitude release the hormone oxytocin, which is very beneficial for you. Oxytocin, which is known as the "bonding hormone" and the "love molecule," contributes to positive feelings of connection and well-being. It has the added benefit of helping to reduce your levels of the stress hormone cortisol.

There are many ways to practice gratitude. Here are a few suggestions:

a. At the end of each day, take a few minutes to write down five things you are grateful for that day. Writing them down is quite important as this enhances the depth of your experience. Try not to repeat any you have written before. Be specific. For instance, don't write "I am grateful for my kids." Instead write something like, "I am grateful for the sound of my children laughing when they watch a funny show." It's especially important to take the time to really *feel* that gratitude for each item on your list.

b. Practice gratitude throughout the day. Look for opportunities to be grateful for small things in your life. For instance you may say to yourself, "I'm grateful for Samantha's smile," and "I'm grateful the sun is shining and the sky is such a deep blue." When you can be grateful for small, everyday

CHAPTER 9

experiences, life starts to seem more special, more of an everyday blessing. Combining gratitude with the body awareness exercise will result in a multiplying effect.

c. Express your gratitude to others. Let people know you appreciate even the small acts of kindness or service they do for you. You will both share in the benefits. Set a goal to express your appreciation to others at least five times per day, and then follow through. For instance, catch your kids "doing something right" and tell them right then and there. They will love it and you probably will too!

For your acknowledgment to have the greatest impact, describe the behavior they did and how it impacted you. For instance, "Steve, I appreciate seeing your smile first thing every morning. You brighten my day!" And, "Thanks for making the coffee this morning; I really love how your coffee tastes. I think you have some kind of magic touch!"

4. Meditate

Extensive research supports the benefits of meditation on health, mental clarity, focus, stress reduction, and resilience to stressors. The "woo-woo" label for meditation has finally worn off, and many of today's most successful people meditate regularly, including CEOs, politicians, prominent doctors, musicians, movie stars, and top athletes. Meditating even for a few minutes will generate positive benefits in relaxing and calming your mind and reducing stress.

Meditation is far simpler than you might think. When you quiet your mind and focus your attention in an observant way, you are meditating.

Sitting on the beach and watching the sunset (without analyzing it or thinking about other things) is a form of meditation. Closing your eyes and listening to beautiful music (without commenting mentally) is a meditation.

There are countless resources available that teach many different forms of meditation. These days, there's something for everyone. I recommend you get started by attending a class, and/or downloading audio recordings or software applications that provide guided meditations. Find a practice you are willing to do every day and stick with it.

You might have guessed that the centering and breathing techniques described above are meditations. Here's another simple meditation you can do for even a minute or two at a time:

   a. Get into a comfortable position in your chair with both feet on the floor and your hands in your lap. Close your eyes.

   b. Take several deep and cleansing belly breaths.

   c. Begin to notice your thoughts. Imagine you are standing in a living area in your home and your thoughts are loud and rowdy children who are demanding your attention. Notice how tiring your thoughts are for you.

CHAPTER 9

    d. Now imagine walking out of the living area into your dark and quiet bedroom and closing the door, blocking out the sound. Imagine sitting on the bed and just enjoy the feeling of peace and quiet. You may still hear your thoughts, but they will be in the distance and easy to ignore.

    e. If a thought intrudes too much, just gently usher it out the door and return to enjoying mental silence.

    f. When the time is right, gently open your eyes and enjoy the sense of relaxed calm.

Managing your stress will help you create a strong foundation for staying resourceful when faced with issues, problems, and other life challenges.

Creating Focused Awareness

Buddhists call the restless mind "monkey mind." The Buddha said the human mind is filled with these monkeys jumping, chattering, and carrying on endlessly. We all have monkey minds with countless monkeys vying for our attention.

Quite a few of my clients report that they think *all the time*. They can't turn their brains off to go to sleep, and they have trouble concentrating on one topic with so many other things on their mind. Do you experience anything like that?

Many people pride themselves on their ability to multi-task and then justify themselves by saying they "have to" multi-task because their job (and life) demands it. Do you notice the drama story here? Their job, or life itself, is the villain that makes them multi-task. The first step in claiming your power is to take responsibility for your behaviors and for making a change. And that's important in this case, because multi-tasking places a large toll on your productivity and stress levels.

> *The first step in claiming your power is to take responsibility for your behaviors and for making a change.*

Earl Miller, MIT professor of neuroscience, asserts, "People can't multitask very well, and when people say they can, they're deluding themselves. For the most part, we simply can't focus on more than one thing at a time. What we can do is shift our focus from one thing to the next with astonishing speed."

That switching doesn't matter if the tasks are routine and do not require much brainpower, like folding clothes while watching a sitcom on television. On the other hand, it matters a lot if the tasks are different and do require thinking, like writing an email and participating in a conversation in a meeting. The brain can't process two significantly different tasks into short-term memory at the same time. As a result, the information can't get transferred to long-term memory, which means you can't or won't remember it.

Scattering your attention is also inefficient. *Inc.* magazine reports multi-tasking can cause a 40 percent drop in your productivity, take you 50 percent longer to complete a task, and introduce up to 50 percent more errors. Heavy multi-tasking can cause you to temporarily lose

CHAPTER 9

15 IQ points—that's 3 times more than the effect from smoking marijuana!

Then there is the price you pay in added stress. The brain finds complex multi-tasking to be stressful and so amps up the stress hormones adrenaline and cortisol. Chronic multi-tasking adds a huge burden to your body's stress load with all of the related health consequences.

So, there are a lot of benefits to be gained from practicing focused awareness.

The breathing exercise described in the prior section is one of the primary practices for developing mindfulness. Especially when you really focus your awareness on the breath, following it as you breathe in and breathe out.

With all of the mindfulness practices, when your mind wanders (and it will), just gently bring your attention back to the matter at hand.

In business, people are commonly preoccupied with multiple subjects at once. Their minds will jump like a monkey from the topic at hand and land on some other pressing topic ... then on to another ... and another ... and finally back to their current task. Then it starts all over again. This is what happens when people can't turn their brain off at night.

The following technique is a powerful visualization that seems to work when other approaches don't. If you are new to using visualizations to influence your subconscious, this may seem a little strange to you. That's normal. It always feels strange, awkward, and even a little embarrassing to try something different for the first time. Can you be okay with that?

Letting Go of Preoccupations

I suggest you combine this technique with some of the other techniques described in this book such as Drain the Pain (which we will talk about in the next chapter) to enhance the overall effectiveness.

1. Close your eyes and become aware of the topics your mind is preoccupied with. Select one topic to begin.

2. Imagine a weighty object like a barbell, rock, or anvil that symbolically represents this topic you have been dwelling on. The size and weight of this object should be relative to the importance and "weight" this topic has had on your mind. Small matters might be imagined as a 2-pound barbell and big ones as a 50-pound barbell.

3. Imagine this weight in your hand. Use all three senses to imagine it vividly. See the color, shape, and size of the weight. Imagine a code word that represents this topic written on the side in a bright color, like "XYZ project." Feel the texture of the object in your hand, the temperature, and the weight as if you were actually holding it.

4. Now imagine dropping it. Letting it drop into water, like dropping it off a boat, is especially effective. Feel the instantaneous release of the weight—feeling much lighter. Hear it splash into the water. See the weight drop away out of sight.

5. Notice the release of some of the tension you may have been holding in your body.

CHAPTER 9

6. Continue to release each of the remaining topics one by one until your mind is clear.
7. Enjoy this clear, quiet state of mind!

Akeela wholeheartedly embraced the mindfulness practices and then taught them to each of her children. Within a few weeks, her blood pressure dropped into the normal range. She slept much better, felt more lighthearted, and did not take matters at work so personally.

Through the preoccupations exercise and other time management techniques, she discovered she could focus much more effectively. Akeela found she achieved more and ended the day with higher energy levels. Also, instead of being distracted by texts and emails during meetings, she gave her employees her full attention. As a result, their communications improved as did their relationships, and the interactions seemed to boost the employees' morale.

All of the children described feeling calmer and less anxious. Zuri noted how much her mood improved and how she generally felt happier. Sophie was more present and aware in her soccer games and was playing her best ever. Because James was more centered and relaxed, his nervous eating declined and he started losing weight. His grades also improved when he was able to remain focused on his homework.

These techniques for achieving mindfulness are powerful and effective, yet they only scratch the surface of all you might learn on this topic. I encourage you to seek out additional materials in books, websites, and videos.

CHAPTER 10

Drain the Pain — From Upset to Calm in 60 Seconds

One of the biggest issues humans have is dealing effectively with pain, especially emotional pain. That's not surprising given we are not really taught how to cope with pain, other than to suppress it.

Thankfully, processing our emotions effectively is easier than you ever imagined.

Drain the Pain is a creative visualization that enables you to quickly and easily release suppressed emotional pain and in some cases even physical pain. By quickly, I mean in less than a minute. Seriously.

> *One of the biggest issues humans have is dealing effectively with pain, especially emotional pain.*

As I describe how to Drain the Pain, take an opportunity to actually use it to release a difficult emotion you are experiencing now. What is bothering, upsetting, or worrying you? Choose a moderate upset until you gain confidence, and then move on to the really big stuff.

I teach this technique to every one of my clients. Most of these senior executives have no experience with visualizations, yet they have all been able to do it successfully. They are almost universally surprised and delighted at the startling difference it makes in such a short time. I predict you will too!

If you are suppressing an emotion, you will feel it in your body somewhere (it has nowhere else to go.) You might feel it as a tension, pressure, or literally as a pain. As you think about something upsetting to you, the physical sensations will often become more intense and easier for you to locate.

We will imagine the emotion is bottled up and can't get out—like it's in a container under pressure. We use *water* as a metaphor for the emotion. The water (emotion) is trying to drain out but can't because it's blocked.

How to Drain the Pain

In Drain the Pain, you will visualize a faucet, spigot, or similar way to drain the "container," and then open it to empty the container. It is *crucial* you use as many senses as you can—vividly see it, hear it, and feel it.

1. Begin by breathing and centering. Breathe deeply from the abdomen. Take several slow deep breaths: in through the nose for 8 counts, hold for 4 counts, and out through the mouth for 8 counts. Repeat at least 3 times, more if needed. This releases tension and increases the clarity of your thoughts.

CHAPTER 10

2. Notice where you feel the emotions in your body. They will feel like a pressure or tension.
3. Imagine a "container" in this area holding a lot of water under pressure (representing your emotions). You might visualize this container as a big cylindrical water tank. Add a clear gauge spanning the container's length so you can monitor the fluid level as it drops. Once you have mastered using the container, you might choose instead to visualize a jug on a water cooler, a beer keg, a teapot, a bathtub or anything else that works well for you.
4. Visualize a "faucet" at the bottom of this container. Mentally reach out and open the faucet, allowing the water to pour out, run through your body and be absorbed into the earth. Watch the gauge to track the water level as it drops all the way down to empty.
   - *It is vital to richly visualize the experience.* This engages the whole brain and is much more convincing to the subconscious. You may want to close your eyes to intensify the experience.
   - Feel your hand turning the faucet. What is the texture? Is it smooth or rough? Does it have a temperature, cool or warm to the touch? Is it easy or difficult to turn? Does it vibrate when the water rushes out? Feel the pressure being released as the water drains out, becoming lighter and lighter until it is all gone.
   - See it happening. See the color, shape, and size of the container. See the faucet; see the

water draining out and being absorbed into the ground. What color is the water? Is it just fluid or is there "dirt" or "debris" being released as well? Let your imagination surprise you!

- Hear the liquid gurgling and splashing as it is released, and maybe even the squeak of the faucet as you open it.

5. Continue until all the sensation of the emotion is relieved.

Notice how much clearer and centered you feel!

Wasn't that amazing? I'm always astounded at how much better I feel after I release the harmful energy.

Drain the Pain is an essential element of *emotional hygiene*. You practice physical hygiene every day, and certain aspects such as hand washing and teeth brushing multiple times each day. I urge you to practice emotional hygiene with the same daily discipline. This is my #1 practice for keeping myself emotionally clean and clear throughout the day.

I recommend you use Drain the Pain every day, even multiple times per day.

- Use it any time you are feeling upset, even if the matter seems minor.
- Use it before bed and you will likely sleep better and feel more rested in the morning.
- Use it on your drive home to let go of your work day and prepare yourself for family time.

CHAPTER 10

- When you feel tension from stress, use Drain the Pain to release the emotions bottled up in your tight muscles.

Sometimes a client reports feeling better, but the release doesn't feel complete. This usually indicates another layer of suppressed emotion, and sometimes multiple layers. My advice is to look further and find where you feel a deeper level of emotion. These might be your personal black sheep emotions. Then repeat *the drain*. Continue until you feel complete, which is when you feel light and open and can't access the emotions from the event any more.

Drain the Pain can even be used to release emotions you have been holding onto for years. Maybe you still feel anger or resentment over a business deal gone bad, or a bad breakup or divorce. When you release the associated emotions, you will find it easier to move past those traumas, to let them go and move on with your life.

Applying Drain the Pain

Many months after being passed over for a promotion, Akeela still felt angry and resentful. So she used my helpful technique to release those emotions.

She started by locating where she felt the emotions in her body. She found them in two areas, in her heart and also a little higher in her chest. The heart area felt heavy, like a weight was on it, while higher in her chest she felt a burning sensation.

She elected to perform the clearing in two steps, starting with the burning sensation. She visualized this as a steam kettle with steam whistling out the top. She tipped it over and poured the steaming water out: seeing, hearing, and feeling it drain out into the earth. As the process completed, the area in her chest cooled off and she felt an expansive sensation instead. This took about 40 seconds.

For the emotion she felt in her heart area, she imagined a big cylinder, like a large water tank. As she started to drain this, she was startled to find the "water" was a dirty dark brown and kind of thick. It took a little longer—about 90 seconds to complete—and while it was processing she started to feel the anger again.

This occasionally happens for me too. Most of the time I don't feel any emotions during the process, which is one of the real benefits. But sometimes I feel anywhere from a tinge to a strong wave of emotion. It's always brief and never too much for me to handle.

Drain the Pain is an essential element of emotional hygiene.

Afterwards, Akeela felt great. I noticed a definite change in her energy, which seemed brighter. Her face had better color and her eyes seemed more open. The muscles in her face were softer and more relaxed and she seemed more comfortable and at ease.

When I asked her to think about the original event—getting passed over for the promotion— she didn't feel anything. She said she was neutral about it. In addition, she surprised both of us when she admitted for the first time she probably hadn't been ready to take on the bigger role! As often happens when we release suppressed

CHAPTER 10

emotions, she viewed the situation quite differently, and saw it in a more mature and effective light. We will explore this phenomenon again when we discuss Max the Moment in Chapter 13.

Akeela introduced Drain the Pain to her family over the next couple of weeks. She had no success in getting her husband Tom to try it out. He laughed at her and ridiculed her suggestion. To understand his reaction, you have to put it into perspective. Due to his lack of employment, Tom is constantly in a highly reactive state. This causes him to be in survival mode—a form of high fear alert and emotional flooding—all the time. Getting someone to try a strange new technique requires enough emotional flexibility to be open-minded and to take a risk. Tom simply did not have that capacity.

Happily, the technique was easy for her son James, who applied it to his anxiety about an upcoming science exam and felt immediate relief. Sophie had an easy time too. She used the technique to let go of the hurt she felt over a girlfriend who betrayed her and then stopped being her friend. After using Drain the Pain, Sophie was delighted to look back on the event and realize she could just let the friendship go and move on.

Younger children—even as young as 6 or 7 years old—have a much easier time with visualizations because they are much more creative and open-minded than most adults.

Akeela's oldest daughter Zuri's efforts were only partially successful. She used the technique to help her prepare for a job interview. Although the feelings of fear, frustration, and self-doubt that had accumulated over the past year from her unsuccessful job-hunting were diminished, they were not completely eliminated. I suggested to Akeela that Zuri might want to try additional "changework" approaches such as Consoling Yourself, which we will discuss in Chapter 12.

Rescuing Yourself from Emotional Hijack

There is a difference between being emotionally "hooked" and being emotionally "hijacked." Emotional flooding is called an *amygdala hijack*. The amygdala is the gland in your midbrain responsible for your fight or flight survival instincts. It can respond to a perceived threat in as little as *12 thousandths of a second*—which is practically instantaneous—and long before your neocortex has even realized something is happening. An amygdala hijack occurs when the fear reaction is so strong you feel overwhelmed.

When you are emotionally *hooked* you can still restore yourself to the pilot seat. Your pilot abandons the driver's seat temporarily but soon returns. However, when *hijacked*, the emotion is SO strong it completely takes you over and you can't influence the reaction at all. Your subconscious takes over the driver's seat and locks you out.

You can tell you have been hijacked because you can't get out of your drama story and you feel panicky. You might also feel like you are about to completely lose control and do something you will regret.

When this happens, create some space for yourself to allow your emotions to cool down. If you continue to try to work through the issue, you are going to do serious

CHAPTER 10

emotional and potentially physical damage to yourself, the other party, and the relationship.

So, call a timeout on yourself and walk away. Get away from the situation and give yourself time to calm down. You can say things like:

- I need a minute to collect myself.
- I need some time to cool off.
- I need some time to think things over.
- We both need to walk away and calm down.

A few of those phrases would be effective in a work setting, but you could also say something like, "Before things get out of hand, I think we should take a break and clear our heads."

Once you walk away, it's *essential* for you to quit dwelling on the drama story since it is the source of your upset in the first place. You have to use every practice you have at your disposal to think about other things, or to clear your mind completely. You especially need to practice deep breathing and Drain the Pain, and it's a great time to use your power phrases.

Once you calm down enough to think more clearly, work the Max the Moment process for yourself *before* re-engaging with the other party. You will be much more successful in making the Pivot to Power to enable a positive resolution.

My father was often angry, and when he disciplined me it was a violent whipping that left welts for days. These were terrifying and agonizing experiences. Later on as an adult, when someone became really angry with me, I would freeze up and panic. Then I would either attack verbally to drive them away or say anything to placate them to get them to calm down and quit being angry. Neither action was a powerful response to the situation. These amygdala hijacks were an obvious result of my childhood experiences.

Once I developed the Inner Mastery system, I was able to recognize what was happening. I would breathe to calm down my panicky feelings and resist acting out in any way. Then I would tell the other person I needed some time to myself. After I calmed down, I was able to go back and work through the issue so that both of us achieved a positive resolution.

CHAPTER 11

Empathic Listening — The Healing Power of Empathic Connection

One of the ways that you can help other people drain their emotional pain is through *empathic listening*.

Have you ever "vented" to someone when you needed to get something off your chest? I read some research on venting and was surprised to learn it actually doesn't work to reduce the emotion, and in fact tends to intensify it. For instance, *Fast Company* magazine reported on a 2013 study titled "Anger on the Internet." Researchers found users of rant sites are more anger-prone in general and more often participate in negative behaviors such as verbal and physical fights, as well as reckless driving. Instead of simply letting off steam, users are fueling their fire.

When people rehash their drama stories, they fire the same neural circuitry that generated the emotions in the first place. Without a release, these emotions can cascade and create emotional flooding.

Empathic listening is a powerful way to help people vent and *truly release* the emotions.

As we discussed in Chapter 6, emotions won't go away until you do something about them. So, when someone is emotionally triggered, you may want to use empathic listening to help them work through it. This is especially important for supporting people without becoming a rescuer, and a key step in resolving conflict and dissolving a Drama Triangle.

> *Empathic listening enables you to help other people drain their emotional pain.*

Imagine emotional upsets are large helium balloons inflated with the bottled-up emotions a person hasn't processed. These balloons are tied to the person and keep getting in the way when they interact with others. The balloons block their view and prevent them from seeing or communicating clearly. They constantly bump into the person and hinder their efforts, increasing their irritation and stress. The balloons also collide with and bruise other people. And no matter how hard the person pushes them away, the balloons keep coming back.

Through empathic listening, you can help them deflate and remove their emotional balloons.

Empathic listening is not about fixing the problem. It is not about listening so you can offer ideas to solve the situation. It is creating an empathic connection through compassionate understanding. This connection enables the other person to reduce or eliminate their emotional charge.

An *empathic connection* is an emotional bond between people who have opened their hearts to

CHAPTER 11

create a shared understanding and appreciation of each others' experiences.

It's virtually impossible to view someone as a villain when you have opened yourself to their pain and their needs and they have done the same for yours. Marshall Rosenberg's classic book *Nonviolent Communication: A Language of Life* relates stories of even mortal enemies—such as Israelis and Palestinians—breaking down the barriers between them through empathic connection.

An Eventful Dinner with Akeela and Tom

Refer back to Chapter 6 where I described the dinner I attended with Akeela and Tom. I had asked Tom some questions about his feelings regarding his failed job interview. My questions emotionally triggered Tom and he abruptly left the room. I believe Tom was in a drama story, feeling like he was being "put on the spot," and afraid of being vulnerable. His emotions were just too much for him on top of everything else he was dealing with regarding his unemployment.

When he returned a few minutes later, I practiced empathic listening with him. Using a gentle voice and demeanor, I said, "Tom, it's clear you have been working really hard to get a job. You know you can make a real contribution to these companies and you are ready to get on with it. I can only imagine how angry and frustrated you must be feeling … and maybe even ashamed about getting turned down yet again." (I was watching his body language closely to make sure my interpretation was accurate, and so far it was.) "And after having been at it this long, you may be feeling some hopelessness and even despair. You probably never imagined it would be this difficult to find a job, or that something like this would ever happen to you. You are a proud man and feel a great responsibility for your family and that might be hardest of all for you—feeling like you let them down."

By the time I stopped talking, Tom's eyes were misting with tears. He looked down at the table and whispered in a husky voice, "I can hardly look them in the eyes ... they must be so ashamed of me." Tears streaked Akeela's face as she reached over and held his hand.

Akeela knew better than to try to fix this for Tom. That's not what he needed. He wanted her to understand the depth of his pain and why he felt that way. So she reflected his reality back to him. She validated him, saying, "I know how hard this is for you. I watch you try and then be rejected over and over again, and yet you pick yourself up and go back and try again. You care so much for your family and so it's especially difficult for you to feel like you have let us down."

It's virtually impossible to view someone as a villain when you have opened yourself to their pain and their needs and they have done the same for yours.

Tom was too choked up to do more than nod "yes." Then Akeela expressed her own feelings. In a grief-soaked voice she said, "When I see you struggle like this ... see you in so much pain ... I feel such sorrow because I want so desperately for you to be happy. I feel so frustrated and angry sometimes! Because I want to help ... and I know that I

CHAPTER 11

can't." At this point, Tom turned toward Akeela and they fell into each other's arms. I made a quiet exit to another room to allow them the time to reconnect and begin mending their broken hearts.

Sometime later, Akeela and Tom entered hand-in-hand to join me in the living room. Frankly, I was astonished—Tom looked like a different man. He looked like the weight of the world had been lifted from his shoulders ... and in a way it had. The color had returned to his cheeks, and his face and eyes were soft and relaxed instead of hard and guarded. He stood upright instead of slightly hunched over. He walked with a relaxed gait instead of the tense "march" he had been doing previously. He smiled and shook my hand and thanked me for my help. And then Tom surprised me again by asking if I would work with him to get a better handle on his emotions. I was thinking, "Finally!" but I just told him I was delighted to help!

I was able to accurately reflect Tom's reality back to him because I had listened deeply not only for his story, but also for his underlying emotions and needs. I "stood in his shoes" long enough to really "get" him and what he was going through. And that is what made this process successful. He was able to break out of his shell and open up about his feelings to Akeela, which paved the way to start healing their relationship. It also opened him up to consider self-development, something he had shown no interest in previously.

Empathic Listening Is Not "Fixing It"

Empathic listening is not about solving a problem or achieving a certain outcome. Rather, it is helping someone process their emotions in a quick and effective way. And once the emotions are out of the way, solutions usually come relatively easily.

When someone is upset and wants to talk about it, they *rarely* want you to solve their problem for them. And if they do want your ideas, they will ask you for them. If you try to solve their problem when they haven't asked for you to do so, that is about you not about them. It is about your need to be the rescuer. If you recognize this pattern in yourself, you might want to consider changing your behavior.

If you hear someone you care about express their emotions and want to stop their hurting, sadness, grief, or anger, this is about you as well. It's a form of rescuing behavior. Those actions are about your discomfort with the pain *you* feel in the presence of their pain. It's fine to draw closer, lean in, and show they have your full attention. Just don't deny them the expression of their emotions.

During a business dinner, I was getting to know an executive team I was about to start working with on a year-long project. I asked each of them to share some thoughts about the difference they wanted to make as a leader in their company. The conversation came around to a huge bear of a man with a reputation for being tough and emotionally distant. He began by describing how important his team was to him. When he revealed how much he cared about them, he began to choke up. Immediately, people began to reach out to him and try to soothe him, patting him on his back and telling him it would be okay. But that was not what he needed or wanted.

He wasn't in pain, he was emotionally moved by the depth of his caring. What he needed was to be understood, to have his deep feelings acknowledged and validated. Their actions were well-meaning but actually served to shut down his expression.

If someone wants to be soothed, they will let you know. Otherwise, the kindest thing you can do is let them have their emotions. Just listen with compassion and seek to understand. Use Drain the Pain if you need to deal with your own reaction, but it may be even better to let your own emotions flow in response. Afterwards, empathic listening can be used to validate their experience.

An Overview of Empathic Listening

Females are generally more naturally empathic listeners, probably because they are often raised to be more nurturing than males. However, I have encountered many hard-driving women executives who immediately jump into problem-solving mode and disregard the empathetic approach. When we first started working together, Akeela was one of these.

Empathic listening includes what is often described as *active listening* but goes much further. Active listening is giving people your undivided attention and providing verbal and body language clues to show you are following along with what they are saying. This is a valuable skill and an integral part of empathic listening.

The goal with empathic listening is to listen in such a way that you can reflect the person's reality—both the facts and the emotions—back to them. You don't agree or disagree. It's not about evaluating or judging their feelings or them in any way. You say you understand them and back it up with the empathic ability to reflect what they are thinking and feeling.

Most people have a profound need to be seen, heard, and understood. They are asking, "Do you get what I'm saying? Can you understand why I think/feel/do what I do?" Empathic listening fulfills those needs.

When you really "get" someone, they almost always feel a tremendous relief, like a burden has been lifted. Referring back to our metaphor, you enable them to "deflate the balloon" they have been carrying around. And you can literally see the relief in their body language—they visibly relax, their skin tone improves, their face and eyes soften, and they will often smile.

In my experience, people frequently follow up my reflection of their story with their own solution for the issue. Or they will say something to put it in perspective, like "Well it's not really a big deal, I'm just going to let it go." People are often perfectly capable of solving their issues once the emotional burden has been released. And if not, they will be much more open to asking for and receiving your help.

When you perform empathic listening correctly, people almost always nod their head in agreement or say

CHAPTER 11

something like, "Yes, that's it." In fact, that's one of the ways you know you have been successful.

Don't worry if you seemed to have misunderstood them; that happens all the time. They will usually correct you right away and then you have another chance to reflect back your understanding. You can use the inquiry phrases described later in this chapter if you need to draw out more information for a better understanding of their situation and emotions.

Reflecting back the other person's reality is called a *paraphrase*. However, it's not the same as is typically taught in business. The business version is much more impersonal and matter-of-fact. It sounds like this: "So, what you are saying is that we need to do three things. One, write a memo documenting the situation; two, have an in-person meeting to discuss the matter; and three, get a commitment for the desired changes. Do I have that correct?" This is a perfect approach when you are dealing with emotionally neutral topics. But if you use that approach with someone who is emotionally charged, they will likely become even more upset.

Empathic listening requires you to *connect with your heart*. Your tones, body language, and words have to communicate your caring. The typical business paraphrasing does not communicate caring, which is why someone would be even more upset. They don't just want your intellectual understanding, they want your compassion for their feelings and for the impact the situation is having on them.

Empathic listening requires you to connect with your heart. Your tones, body language, and words have to communicate your caring.

This style of listening takes more time, effort, and skill, but the payoff is huge. People feel substantially better afterwards—and so do you! Empathic listening helps reduce their stress, improves their productivity and creativity, and increases their resourcefulness (restores some of their personal power). In addition, it strengthens your relationship—the bond between you will be stronger. Connection like this releases the powerful hormone oxytocin (for both of you), which is the bonding molecule. This leads to increased cooperation (especially related to challenging requests), better communication between the two of you, and a greater willingness to forgive if you do something to offend.

What If You Don't Care About Their Feelings?

The key to empathic listening is demonstrating a caring attitude. But what do you do if you don't actually care about the other person's feelings? I have been asked, "If I don't really care, should I fake it?" And the answer is, "Of course not." But you do need to find a way to validate that their feelings matter. At a minimum, doing so will be helpful to you in achieving your outcomes.

You might start by examining your reasons for *not* caring. Part of our human nature is to care about other people. We are born literally wired for empathy. Our brains have *mirror neurons*, which give us the capability to instinctively and immediately understand what other people are experiencing. This is the reason a crying baby will cause the other babies nearby to begin crying as well.

CHAPTER 11

If you aren't experiencing empathy for another person, there's a reason you have closed off your heart. The cause lies within you, and it's reducing your resourcefulness and diminishing your effectiveness in relating to other people.

Obviously, there could be many reasons you don't care about another person's feelings. One of the most common is you have numbed your sensitivity to a particular person. Feeling upset with someone will often cause you to lose empathy for them.

Part of our human nature is to care about other people. We are born literally wired for empathy.

At the extreme end of this spectrum, sociopaths have no empathy for anyone. Also, severe prejudice or hate can lead people to feel no empathy for the objects of their enmity. And that can lead to harmful acts against others. As I write this, the world is reeling from a mass murder where a lone gunman snuffed out the light of dozens of innocent souls. Just because they were gay. When we close off our heart, we lose touch with our humanity, the light of our soul.

If you are struggling to feel empathy for someone specific, I suggest you perform Drain the Pain for yourself prior to attempting empathic listening. However, learning about another person's pain and the needs that drive them may be enough to soften your heart. Akeela had been dealing with conflicts and hard feelings with Tom for months prior to our dinner conversation, and yet, feeling his pain melted her frozen heart in just moments.

If you generally don't care about other people's feelings, then you might have shut down your heart as a defensive mechanism. If this is a possibility, you might want to examine the ways you are numbing yourself—through some addictive or compulsive behavior or by simply suppressing your feelings.

In either case, this deficiency is limiting your effectiveness and the quality of your life. Opening your heart requires the willingness and ability to face your own pain and deal with it effectively. Many of the practices in this book can help you with this. However, please don't hesitate to get additional help through therapy or life coaching.

It may save your life one day. Having a "hardened heart" isn't just a colorful description; it can become reality and lead to severe health issues. *The Huffington Post* reports on a study conducted by the Harvard School of Public Health and University of Rochester psychologists, which found suppressing emotions increases the risk of dying from heart disease and certain forms of cancer. They go on to say, "The health risks increase, it seems, when people have no way of expressing or acting on their feelings …"

How to Listen Empathically

There are two parts to empathic listening: inquiry and reflection.

Step 1: Inquiry — The purpose of inquiry is to understand the person's drama story, their emotions (the pain they are experiencing), and their underlying needs. What they need from you will always be the same: *understanding*, *compassion*, and *validation*. Their needs with regard to their drama story will vary based on the situation.

CHAPTER 11

In this phase, you are gathering information like a good news reporter. You need to be as objective as possible. Capture their communication as they meant it—accurately and without judgment or embellishment.

In a casual conversation, the other person may pour out their story in such a way that you have no need to ask additional questions. This is rarely the case in a business setting.

Your questions will be most effective when you ask "how" and "what" rather than "why" questions. "Why" questions will almost always cause an emotionally charged person to become defensive. Just consider how you feel when someone asks you, "Why did you do that?!!" Besides, "how" and "what" questions reveal much more useful information anyway.

Also, be sure to ask open-ended questions. This way, people will reveal what is important to them. In contrast, closed-ended questions are commonly used to control the conversation, and that might put someone on the defensive as well.

Close-ended questions force people into short or yes/no responses. Close-ended questions sound like:

- Did you consider asking them why we should give them a discount when nobody else gets one?
- Did you want them to admit they were wrong?

In contrast, open-ended questions would be:
- How did you handle it when they asked for a discount?
- What did you want from them?

Some questions are not questions at all, but a backhanded way to make a statement. These are questions like: "Don't you think ..." or "Wouldn't you agree ..." Or, for example, "Don't you think we should spend Christmas with my parents this year?" These are certainly not appropriate for empathic listening, or maybe ever.

Because your questions might feel invasive, consider starting off with a declaration of your positive intentions. Then the other person will understand your motivations. Your positive intent expresses what you are committed to in this interaction. Consider something like this:

- Your concerns are important to me, so ...
- I really value our relationship, so I want to understand ...
- I care about your well-being, so ....
- I'm committed to your success ...

Here are some useful questions you might use to gather quality information and promote cooperation:

- Can you help me understand ...?
- What is your viewpoint on this?
- How do you see this situation?
- Will you talk me through the situation/your understanding?
- Can you say some more about that?
- Could you please clarify what you mean by ... ?
- How so?

CHAPTER 11

- Such as?
- Like what?
- What else?

To understand their emotions:
- What emotions came up for you?
- How did that make you feel?
- How did you feel about that?

To understand their needs in a particular situation:
- What were you hoping for ... ?
- What were you wanting to get from ... ?
- What was important to you about ... ?
- What did you need from ... ?
- What would getting that outcome do for you?
- What concerned you about ... ?

Sometimes you might need to soften these questions more by adding a *buffer phrase* at the beginning, such as "I am wondering if ..." or " Would you be willing to say ..." This is usually necessary when someone is either highly triggered or untrusting of you or the process.

Step 2: Reflection — This step is the heart of empathic listening because you demonstrate your compassionate understanding. Including information both about the situation and the person's feelings is important to achieve the full benefit.

You can perform the reflection in small snippets as the conversation progresses, or you can wait until the person is finished talking and relate the entire story back at once.

My interaction with Tom at dinner was the latter case as is Akeela's example under Applying Empathic Listening.

Here are some examples of reflecting on pieces of a conversation.

Statement 1: That job requisition has been sitting on someone's desk for three weeks—three weeks! Meanwhile, the work keeps piling up!

Reflection: Sounds like you're *really* frustrated and ready to get on with the work.

Statement 2: My brother is coming to visit, and I am dreading it. All he does is complain and criticize the whole time he is here.

Reflection: Well sure, you want his visit to be enjoyable but you're afraid it won't be.

Statement 3: I'm excited about moving to Seattle for my new job, but then I think about packing up all that junk that has been piling up for years and I'm dreading it!

Reflection: Seems like it's bittersweet for you. You're really excited about the job but the move seems overwhelming.

When you reflect someone's story back to them, the key is to relate the story from *their perspective*—NOT from your interpretation of the situation. There may be a role for your interpretation later, but not at this point in the process. Here are some examples of an accurate reflection followed by an incorrect reflection distorted by the listener's BIAS.

CHAPTER 11

<u>Statement 1</u>: My team is really working well together, but I have one person who almost seems to take pleasure in getting into arguments with other people.

Correct Reflection: You're pretty happy with your team but frustrated that one person can't seem to get along with others.

Incorrect Reflection: You might need to fire that person who is screwing up your team.

<u>Statement 2</u>: I'm so angry! My father was just diagnosed with cancer and my mother—the drama queen—is freaking out and making it all about herself.

Correct Reflection: I understand, you are fed up with your mother because you really want to focus on supporting your father right now but she is making that difficult.

Incorrect Reflection: Your mother is really being selfish.

Your reflection can include some of their drama story so long as you don't communicate you are agreeing or disagreeing with it.

<u>Statement 1</u>: I'm never going to get a fair chance to get promoted, not as long as Stephen has a grudge against me.

Correct Reflection: You are feeling bitter and disappointed because you really want that job but are convinced the deck is stacked against you.

Incorrect Reflection: You are angry because you are getting screwed in this deal.

<u>Statement 2</u>: I can't believe my parents were so cheap they wouldn't pay for my college. All my friends have

their college paid for. Now I'm going to have to find a way to pay off a ton of debt.

Correct Reflection: You think it's unfair for you to have all this college debt while others get off without having to pay a penny. And you are angry because you expected more support from your parents.

Incorrect Reflection: You are pissed off that you have a lot of debt and other people don't, but hey, your parents don't owe you anything.

Applying Empathic Listening

Once she learned empathic listening, Akeela mastered it quickly. I witnessed her using this technique in a meeting I was monitoring. One of her employees, "Tracy," was extremely angry over a matter and his negative attitude was affecting his work and rubbing off on his co-workers.

Akeela started the conversation by saying she wanted to reassure Tracy that she supported him and wanted to help find a positive resolution to this situation. Then she asked, "Can you help me understand what happened?"

Tracy related that a person in another department, Zack, had lied to him and caused Tracy to miss the due date for a special customer analysis. Zack then betrayed him by telling the department head Tracy had been rude and inappropriate with him over the phone. Tracy denied ever doing that.

Akeela did not have any information about this matter other than what Tracy was relaying. She did not know one way or another if Tracy's story was true. Clearly,

CHAPTER 11

Tracy was portraying himself as the innocent victim in this drama story. Akeela knew not to buy into it, and she certainly wasn't going to be his rescuer.

She listening attentively as Tracy told his story. She nodded her head, made sounds like "um hmmm," made appropriate eye contact, and asked clarifying questions when she didn't understand. When it seemed Tracy was done, Akeela reflected his story back to him.

Akeela said, "Here's what I heard. You were just trying to get your job done. You have this major report to get out to senior management by the deadline and it was really important to you to get it done well and on time. You depended on Zack in accounting to get you the information he promised. As the deadline approached, you say you did the responsible thing and called him to find out what was going on. Zack then denied you had ever asked for the information in the first place. You thought you handled the call well, but then you heard Zack had reported to the department head you had mistreated him. You are really angry and frustrated with all this. You feel betrayed and dealt with unfairly. Also, you are embarrassed about submitting the report late. And I'm guessing that's really hard on you because you pride yourself on doing good work."

And then she paused. Tracy sat there for a moment and then looked down, nodded his head 'yes' and with a big sigh said, "Yeah, that's pretty much it." Tracy looked relieved.

Akeela allowed the silence to stretch out. Then Tracy said. "Well, I guess I need to go talk with Zack and straighten this out. Do you have any advice for me?"

The quality of Akeela's listening not only enabled Tracy to get over his upset, it helped him open up to receive feedback. Once she was invited to do so, Akeela talked with him about his drama story and the consequences it caused. She helped him own his role in the breakdown and describe what he would do differently next time. Then they explored and agreed to options for resolving the situation with Zack and the department head.

> Opening your heart requires the willingness and ability to face your own pain and deal with it effectively.

What a victory for Akeela! Her measured, kind approach showed the maturity Mr. Singh the CEO felt she lacked before. She was able to show empathy rather than harshness. Plus, she didn't have to get in the middle of the dispute between Tracy and Zack and micromanage the situation.

CHAPTER 12

Consoling Yourself — Be Your Own Knight in Shining Armor

You can use empathic listening to help yourself get over an upset you otherwise can't stop dwelling on. In this way, you provide yourself with self-love and compassionate understanding.

When Drain the Pain Isn't Enough

Sometimes you may feel so upset about an issue you can't let it go. You may have used Drain the Pain, and yet the emotions keep coming back. Your mind just keeps going over and over the situation.

In these circumstances, talking it out so you can truly be heard and understood provides a perfect opportunity for empathic listening. If someone can provide it for you, great. If not, knowing how to provide empathic listening for yourself can be a big help. When you need a "knight in shining armor," you can be there for yourself!

Often, these sorts of persistent upsets occur because the current issue in your adult life has triggered the memory of a similar episode from your childhood. Your subconscious is reacting to the current event the way you did to the event when you were, let's say, 3 years old. A three-year-old may cry hysterically, throw herself on the ground, scream in anger and frustration, lash out, and thrash around when you try to hold her. We've all seen it, right? Children behave like this because they don't know how to handle what they are feeling. Your inner child is experiencing the same thing, right now, in reaction to what's happening in your current life.

If you're a parent, you have likely experienced times when your child was so upset they were completely out of control. When it happened, you stepped in and consoled them until they could calm down enough to come back to their senses. You do this same thing, except you do it for yourself.

You talk to yourself using reassuring third-person language. Consoling yourself is most effective when you handle the situation as an adult comforting a child having an emotional reaction. But you can imagine whatever combination (adult/child, adult/adult) works best for you.

You may feel silly the first time you do this. But be patient with yourself; the benefits truly can be remarkable.

As before, this visualization is most effective when you create a vivid experience that engages all three senses. In this example, I will use male pronouns, for no other reason than to avoid the awkward use of the neutral "them." I will also describe this assuming you will be speaking with a child; simply substitute an adult if you prefer.

CHAPTER 12

If you are aware of a current upset you can't seem to move beyond, you can use that for this exercise. Otherwise, consider an unresolved situation from your past. Practically everyone has an emotional upset in their history that hasn't fully healed. Take a moment to see if you can locate something like that from your past.

How to Console Yourself

Here are the steps to follow:

1. Close your eyes and turn your attention inward.
2. Begin by using Drain the Pain.
3. Now, allow your creative imagination to show you a visual representation of your inner child who is upset. Imagine the scene as if it were occurring in real life. Notice how the child is behaving, which emotions he seems to be experiencing.
4. Have your child-self tell you what is upsetting him. Use empathic listening—listen with unconditional love and compassion. Hold him in your lap while he talks if it feels right to you.
5. This step is different with a child vs. an adult. Once you have listened and validated him, say what is needed to comfort the child. Keep it simple. Say "I love you," and "it will be okay," and similar comforting statements.
6. Once he seems complete with talking about the event, your child-self will almost always want physical comfort, just like a real child would. Bring your

inner child into your arms and hold him in your lap (if you haven't already done so). Comfort him with gentle words, kisses, stroking his head or back, and holding him tight (just as you might have done with your own children). Continue this process until it seems the reaction has been fully processed.

When a child is done with being upset, they are really done. They are ready to get down and return to playing ... and they will tell you so! They don't dwell on the upset and don't look back. That will happen in this visualization as well.

7. When the child is complete with the process, set him down and let him go off to play.
8. Scan your feelings. If any lingering emotions need to be released, use Drain the Pain.
9. Open your eyes and return to full waking consciousness.

As with any other skill you learn, you will get better with practice. In fact, you will probably get to a point where you can perform this effortlessly and in less than a couple of minutes. And sometimes even in a matter of seconds.

Imagine that! Being able to release something in a matter of minutes you may have been carrying around with you for years or even decades!

CHAPTER 12

Applying the Console Yourself Practice

After learning this skill for herself, Akeela asked me to work with her daughter. Zuri was struggling with her emotions because she had been unsuccessful getting a job. I was glad to do so, and talked Zuri through the process.

Zuri was able to quickly see an image of her younger self. She estimated the little girl was probably 4 years old. In Zuri's imagination, Little Zuri was huddled up with her knees to her chest and was holding a comfort blanket, rocking back and forth with a glazed look in her eyes.

At first, the adult Zuri started to get choked up from feeling the emotions of the little girl. So I asked her to mentally separate herself from the emotions and let Little Zuri be the one to express them. She did that, and then imagined approaching her younger self and squatting down beside her. She asked young Zuri to tell her what was wrong. "Mommy's gone … I don't know where she is … She don't love me anymore," she said in a small voice.

[After her parents had divorced, Zuri's mother disappeared from her life. Like most children who don't know any better, Zuri assumed it was her fault and her mother left because she did not love her. The fear of being left all alone and not knowing what to do overwhelmed her. She also felt both guilty and terribly hurt. In present time, those old feelings were triggered by the similar situation of graduating college (being all alone) and not being able to get a job (they don't love me).]

Adult Zuri imagined gently picking up young Zuri and cuddling her in her lap. She held her to her chest and validated her: "You are so scared and hurt, and you feel like you are all alone. Your mommy went away and you don't know why. You are afraid it's your fault and that your mommy left because she didn't love you anymore. And I know it still hurts you so much!"

Little Zuri clutched her in a death grip and then started to cry—she sobbed because her heart had been broken into a million pieces. Adult Zuri just held her, rocking gently and stroking her hair and making soothing sounds. She told Little Zuri, "I love you … it'll be okay."

Imagine that! Being able to release something in a matter of minutes you may have been carrying around with you for years or even decades!

As I watched from beside her, tears started to roll down Zuri's cheeks. She could not help feeling profound compassion for the pain her younger self was feeling. That's a common experience when you have an open heart and comfort someone in profound pain.

After another minute, Zuri reported that young Zuri had stopped crying and fallen asleep in her arms. She held her and continued to comfort her for a minute or so. Then Little Zuri roused herself and asked to be set down, and then ran off to play.

After Zuri opened her eyes, she didn't want to talk about the experience for a couple of minutes. It was extremely moving for her and she just wanted to sit quietly with it for a bit. When she was ready to talk, Zuri told me she realized how much she loved her little girl and then choked up again.

After a few more minutes, she felt better. I asked her to think about the upcoming interview and her job hunting

CHAPTER 12

process. Zuri laughed! Then she smiled and shook her head and said, "I can't believe it. I feel great about it and I'm excited about finding a job instead of dreading it!"

Zuri's experience was a little more intense than most you will normally encounter. After all, she confronted a colossal emotional wound and then processed through it in less than 10 minutes. As always, I was humbled and awed to participate in such a magnificent act of courage, love, and healing. I am so grateful to be able to do this work!

As a postscript, Zuri did not get the job, but she did get hired for the one after that. "It isn't my dream job," she told me, "but I can see it from here!"

CHAPTER 13

Max the Moment — Be Your Best When the "Chips Are Down"

Akeela made a lot of improvement in managing her emotions and behaviors using the practices we have discussed thus far. Her stress stayed mainly in the green (calm) zone, and she did a good job processing her emotions effectively. She witnessed the benefits in how she felt, the quality of her interactions and relationships with others, and the positive feedback she received from her co-workers and children.

Even so, sometimes a situation would trip an emotional trigger and Akeela would act out in some negative way—often even before realizing she was upset. By then, the damage was done. She then had to circle back with people to apologize and mend hurt feelings. I explained the importance of managing these reactions because of the significant repercussions on her and others.

Taking the High Road

In order to lead a great life, you need to be your best when things are toughest. Regrettably, that's when you are most likely to launch into a drama story and react in a negative and forceful manner.

Imagine two leaders facing a crisis. They just learned a product shipped with a significant design flaw. One leader blows up and starts screaming at people, looking for someone to blame, humiliating and shaming in the process. The second leader takes a moment to digest the news and calm themselves. Then they convene a meeting and mobilize everyone to focus on the solution—to assess the right thing to do and to look for creative solutions.

- For whom would you rather work?
- Which of the leaders orchestrated the most effective and efficient solution to the crisis?
- How did the employees of the different leaders feel about themselves? The situation? The leader?

If you said you'd rather work for the second leader, you're not alone. Highly talented people charged with leading others often have great technical skills and talents. However, many have never developed the ability to manage their emotions under stressful circumstances. It's about so much more than generating results any way you can. Your leadership style impacts people's morale, mental state, creativity, confidence, and much more.

Can you see how an executive team full of leaders and managers with high emotional intelligence could help your business in countless ways?

CHAPTER 13

Similar challenges occur for parents, like when your child has been involved in some mischief. Recall from Chapter 10 the way Tom and Akeela handled the incident when Sophie was suspended from school. Their behavior in the situation led to a major upset for everyone, especially for Sophie.

Couples face their own challenges when they disagree or fight over some matter. Imagine this scenario: a spouse didn't balance the checkbook and so bounced a check; their negligence cost them a lot of money in fees and penalties. What's likely to happen here? Is the situation going to devolve into a reactive mess? Or will someone rise above the drama and take the high road?

> *In order to lead a great life, you need to be your best when things are toughest.*

When two people butt heads and engage in drama (the "low road"), they will struggle and make little progress. However, the situation can be transformed when one of them chooses an emotionally mature response (the "high road"). Choosing the high road creates the potential for positive resolution of the conflict.

Are you willing to be the one who chooses the high road?

Max the Moment enables you to quickly Pivot to Power in dealing with an upset. You can use this life skill to transform your reactions into positive and productive outcomes for all the parties involved.

"Throwing the Switch" to a Creative Response

Have you seen movies or cartoons showing a railroad track that splits into two separate tracks? A lever just before the split controls which track the train will travel down. For your hot button reactions, the lever is stuck in the position that takes you down the track to drama and upset. Every time you experience one of your triggering events, your emotional "train" travels down the track to "Dramatown." Through Max the Moment, you will "throw the lever" to the other track—to mentally take yourself down the creative track to a productive response.

The key to Max the Moment is transferring authority from the autopilot to the pilot. You move from a first-person viewpoint (being *immersed* in the drama) to a third-person perspective (*observing* the drama). You accomplish this through depersonalizing the event. Control is then transferred from your emotional mid-brain to the rational pre-frontal cortex—from the autopilot to the pilot.

This shift is similar to waking from a dream. When you are fully dreaming, you are a player in the dream. But when you realize you are the *dreamer* who is *having* a dream, you pop out of it. It quits being a dream and becomes a fantasy you are controlling.

When you are a player in the drama, you are in it and don't have any power over it. You are one or more of the drama story roles. When you name the drama and disengage from it, you re-engage the pre-frontal cortex and regain the power to choose. You quit being a *player* in the drama and become an *observer* who can opt out of the drama.

CHAPTER 13

Overview of Max the Moment

When you first learn Max the Moment, it may seem like a lot to think about while you are really upset. In the beginning, it may take you a little longer to be able to respond appropriately to a dramatic situation. As you gain experience though, Max the Moment will become second nature and you will barely have to think about it to regain your composure.

In summary, Max the Moment goes like this: ***Tame It, Name It, Reframe It.***

Tame It — Recognize you are having an emotional reaction. Take responsibility for your reaction and stop yourself from acting out in a negative way. Use deep breathing to reduce your stress reaction and then use Drain the Pain to neutralize your emotions and make it easier to choose a positive response.

Name It — Describe your drama story and note your emotions. Identify your underlying needs in this situation.

Reframe It — Gain clarity about and focus on your desired outcome. Describe what really happened, without judgment or embellishment, and challenge your assumptions. If another party is involved, seek to understand their perspective by "standing in their shoes." Then create an empathic connection to open the door for mutually beneficial outcomes.

Once you learn Max the Moment, you will be able to adapt it easily to each specific situation. You don't have to do all the steps in every situation or follow them in this specific order. In many cases, you will resolve the reaction before you complete all the steps, and sometimes even in the first step!

For instance, simply draining the emotion (Step 1) might be enough to enable you to choose a creative response. In another situation, you might jump straight to focusing on your outcome (Step 3). As a third example, you might immediately recognize the emotion you are feeling and make a request for what you need (Step 2).

The following description is highly detailed to help you master the material. People are complex, and trite solutions usually don't work. However, actually using Max the Moment is often fast and quite simple.

Remember, the goal is "*progress* not *perfection*" in being able to do this effectively.

Step 1 — Tame It

In this portion of Max the Moment, you will recognize when you are getting emotionally triggered and quickly process through it. Getting upset is like getting "hooked" by your drama story. Like a fish that has taken the bait and found an unwelcome hook inside, you want to "throw the hook" as quickly as you can.

Recognize you are having an emotional reaction. First, you have to realize you are in a reaction in order to be able to take charge and transform it. That's not always easy. Fortunately, there are several ways you can become aware you are having an emotional reaction.

CHAPTER 13

Notice you are feeling an emotion. You may recognize immediately you are feeling angry, frustrated, offended, sad, or a host of other emotions. If so, you are emotionally triggered and in a reactive state.

Notice the physical reactions in your body. What bodily sensations do you typically experience that can alert you to an emotional reaction? Examples include: your face becoming hot or flushed, clenching your jaw or fists, grinding your teeth, tears welling up, unable to find words, stammering, clenching in your stomach or abdomen, or tightness in your chest.

Notice your negative internal self-talk. Your negative self-talk could be fearful like: "I'm in trouble now"; angry like: "I'm not going to take this"; judgmental like name calling: "What a jerk"; victim like: "Why does she always pick on me?" or something else similar to these.

Notice you are behaving poorly. Another sign is acting impulsively without thinking about the appropriate way to respond. For example, being blunt to the point of being offensive or snapping off a sarcastic or hurtful comment.

Notice when you seek out a "rescuer." This refers to occasions when you seek out a distraction to relieve or numb your feelings—especially when you need to be focused elsewhere and know that element of distraction isn't best for you. Examples include indulging a food craving, checking social media, stopping what you are doing to play a video game, escaping into a good book, grabbing an alcoholic drink, and any other addictive, compulsive, or dramatic behavior you habitually do.

Interrupt the reaction so you don't act it out on others. For example, say "Stop!" or "Hold on now!" in your mind to interrupt the emotion, or call a "time-out" in your mind. Some people wear a rubber band on their wrist and snap it when they feel a reaction coming on. Acknowledge to yourself you are reacting by mentally saying something like "I'm triggered," or "I'm hooked."

Getting upset is like getting "hooked" by your drama story. Like a fish that has taken the bait and found an unwelcome hook inside, you want to "throw the hook" as quickly as you can.

Research indicates self-talk is much more effective when you use your own name. So, instead of saying "I am triggered," I might say, "Okay Mark, you're triggered!" Try both versions and determine what works best for you.

Take responsibility for your reaction. Remember: your thoughts, emotions, and behaviors are generated within you. Taking responsibility shifts the power to choose your response away from the situation and back to you. This shift helps put you into creator mode.

Use a power phrase like "This is about me," or "This is my 'stuff'." Or you can phrase it as a vote of confidence like "I can handle this," "I get to choose," or "I'm taking the high road!" In third-person, it might sound something like "Mark, get a grip; you are in charge here."

Use Drain the Pain to release your emotions. This is the same technique you learned earlier.

Recall that the first step is to breathe deeply. My dear friend, Denise Whitney, PhD., the voice and wisdom of Dr. Savvy Speaks, teaches others to first breathe and be

CHAPTER 13

in the present moment. She has developed the ability to stop in the moment of any upsetting reaction using the mantra "just breathe." This thought brings her fully into the present moment and empowers her to choose a positive action to take.

The second part of this process is to identify where you carry the suppressed emotion in your body. Then use a creative visualization to drain and release it.

When I first developed Drain the Pain, I was surprised by a positive side effect from draining the emotion. I found the drama story lost most, if not all, of its hold on me and I was able to much more easily shift into a positive response.

> For instance, I was driving home from a shopping trip to the grocery store. I was recovering from an injury that was slow to heal and painful when I walked. I was pretty frustrated at this point because the shopping trip had been a painful ordeal.
>
> So I started to feel sorry for myself and suddenly thought, "Wouldn't it be great to stop and get a frozen yogurt on the way home? And adding some chopped pecans would make it even better!" I could almost taste the yummy deliciousness of this sweet indulgence and my mood started to improve right away.
>
> And that's when I realized I was engaging in a compulsive behavior to numb my emotional pain. My injury was persecuting me and I was seeking out a sugary snack to rescue me. I immediately started to breathe deeply and used Drain the Pain. I wasn't draining the physical pain but the psychological one of feeling sorry for myself.

As soon as the emotions were gone, I thought about getting yogurt and was completely uninterested. I thought, "I don't want all that sugar ... and I'm not even hungry. Besides, I need to get home and don't really have the time to stop." With that realization, I promptly forgot about even wanting to get yogurt and made my way home.

Those sudden shifts are amazing to me! I experience that sort of detachment practically every time I use Drain the Pain.

Step 2 — Name It

Recall from our earlier conversation that naming your drama story and emotions is a potent way to Pivot to Power—to transfer control from your autopilot to your pilot.

Ultimately, the formula for the Name It step is this:

My story is that (persecutor) is (thwarting/threatening/harming) me.

And so I am feeling (emotions).

Because what I need is (needs).

Example 1

The company is cheating me by not paying my overtime.

I'm angry and disgusted with them because ...

I need be able to trust the company.

CHAPTER 13

<u>Example 2</u>

My wife is making me do the dishes and she knows it's making me miss my football game.

I'm really bitter and resentful because ...

I need the freedom to choose what I do with my time.

<u>Example 3</u>

The grid is down and if I can't locate the supervisor at the plant I'm going to catch hell.

I'm frustrated and worried because ...

I need to be able to do my job and stay out of trouble.

Describe your drama story. Answer these questions about your drama story:

- Who is the villain in your story?
- How have you been thwarted, threatened, or harmed?

Name your emotions. This is simply labeling the emotion(s) you are feeling such as "I'm angry and frustrated." If you can't get in touch with specific emotions, then you can use general terms like "upset" or "bothered."

There may be deeper emotions in this situation that aren't so obvious. Identifying your black sheep emotions will help you pinpoint important needs. To identify these emotions, you have to dig deeper than the first emotion that pops into your mind. Think about each of your personal black sheep emotions and see if any apply.

Identify your needs. This may not be as easy as it sounds. Instead of needs, what people often identify are the behaviors they want from other people to fix their pain. These may sound like:

- I need for her to apologize.
- I need my boss to stop criticizing me.
- I need the kids to pick up after themselves.
- I need the babysitter to be more responsible.

Those might be valid *outcomes* for a given situation, but those are not the underlying *needs*.

The need is an *internal experience*. Here is a partial list of needs:

safety, closeness, intimacy, connection, support, belonging, integrity, acceptance, trust, love, appreciation, understanding, meaning, achievement, dignity, respect, choice, freedom, excitement, creativity, challenges, harmony, enjoyment, affection, validation

If you struggle to identify your underlying needs, you can ask yourself a simple question.

What do I want to experience in this situation that is missing?

Here's an example:

> Tom was angry that Akeela worked late every night for what seemed like months. He lashed out at her, accusing her of caring more about work than her family.
>
> When we first discussed his reaction, Tom said his need was for Akeela to *work fewer hours and be home more*. I pointed out this was actually the *solution* to what he thought was the problem, not his real need.

CHAPTER 13

I asked Tom, "What do you want to experience in this situation that is missing for you?" He answered immediately, "*Companionship, to spend some time alone together and feel like a couple again.*"

What Tom was *doing* was criticizing his wife for working too hard and not caring about the family, but what he *needed* was her companionship and intimacy. His original solution—for her to work fewer hours—would not guarantee his needs would be met. She could work fewer hours and still not spend time with him. Also, it's quite possible for her to continue to work long hours and for them to work out how they can *also* spend some intimate time together.

You might notice how counterproductive Tom's behavior was for getting what he really needed. Lashing out at her is much more likely to push her further away.

Here's another example:

Carmen complained about her brother-in-law mistreating her sister. Apparently, he constantly used abusive language, criticized her, and embarrassed her in front of other people. When describing this, Carmen was visibly upset, cursing him and calling him all sorts of derogatory names. At first she identified her need as "*I need him to treat my sister right—with caring and respect.*"

Then I asked her what she wanted to experience that was missing for her.

She replied, "*I hurt so much seeing my sister abused like that. I want the pain to go away.*"

What Carmen was **doing** was criticizing and belittling her brother-in-law, which ironically is what he was doing to her sister, but what she **needed** was to heal her emotional pain. Carmen knows she can't fix this situation for her sister, but she has not been able to deal with her feelings about it. That's what she needs help with.

But Carmen's constant complaining and badmouthing her brother-in-law was turning people off and pushing them away. If instead she would talk about her feelings and how much pain she was in, people would be much more willing to support her.

And one more example:

Denny has an employee named Sheran who has struggled in her job. She has consistently missed deadlines and the quality of her work is often not up to par. Denny finally got fed up and has started jumping in and doing the work himself. Now he is finding himself stretched too thin and feeling a lot more stress. In addition, Sheran has been complaining to people that Denny is micromanaging her.

Denny considered what he wanted to experience that was missing for him. He realized it was *trust—he needed to be able to trust Sheran to do her job effectively.*

What Denny was *doing* was jumping in and doing the work himself. But what he *needed* was to be able to trust Sheran's work. His solution—to do it himself—was doing nothing to fulfill his need. Instead, he realized he needed to get Sheran some training and coaching, which would enable her to improve her performance.

CHAPTER 13

This situation may seem obvious to you from your outsider's viewpoint. But in my experience, this behavior happens frequently at every level of management.

People who are in reaction mode rarely take actions that fulfill their real needs. Ironically, their actions often produce the opposite of what they want.

Tom needed intimacy but his actions were further alienating Akeela. Carmen needed emotional healing but her behaviors were pushing people away. Denny needed to trust Sheran to do her job but his actions were making her less effective.

Once you identify your real needs, you can choose positive behaviors that can fulfill those needs.

Step 3 — Reframe It

Reframing the situation involves intentionally changing how you see it and choosing a productive response. A "frame" is a mental filter, part of your BIAS, which causes you to view and react to a situation in a certain way.

Imagine that a mental frame is like a window. Every time you look out the window, you see the same situation in the same way. If the frame is your reactor orientation, you will always see a villain out that window, which will lead to drama.

However, if you turn and look out a different window—a creator frame—you will see the scene in a very different way. Instead of a villain, you may see this as

> *Reframing the situation involves intentionally changing how you see it and choosing a productive response.*

merely a *challenge* that you need to handle in order to get your desired outcome. This *reframe* gives you substantially different possibilities for action and for creating positive outcomes. Here's a personal example:

> At a recent family reunion, my elderly mother was watching the news on the television with the volume turned up quite loud. We hardly ever have a TV on in my home and *never* watch the news. I don't like the droning sound of the TV and the news is always so negative and slanted I don't want to engage with it. So, I became more and more annoyed and resentful at my mother having this "trash" (my label) on the TV, which was disrupting our nice family visit. I realized this reactor frame was souring my attitude and ruining my experience, so I wondered to myself, "How can I see this in a creative way?" I thought about how happy it made my mother to follow a routine and especially to watch the news. My mother's happiness is important to me. So I decided to change the label I was using. This wasn't "an intrusive and annoying noise," instead it was the *"sound of my mother's happiness."* The moment I came up with that new way of looking at the situation, the TV ceased to bother me!

There are several important reframes in this step:

- Shift from a problem orientation to an outcome focus.
- Shift from your interpretation to the objective facts of the situation and challenge your assumptions.
- Shift from "villainizing" the other party to seeing the situation from their perspective.

CHAPTER 13

Identify what outcome(s) you want in this situation. The reactor frame focuses on the *problem*, with the mindset "this problem shouldn't be happening." It's the view something is *wrong* here. This frame invokes a judgment, which will invariably lead to a drama story and subsequently a reaction.

The creator frame focuses on the *desired outcome*. This shift to an outcome orientation has a profound impact on people's mindsets and emotions. When the focus is on something being *wrong*, people will automatically begin to take actions to keep themselves safe. They don't want the shame or punishment from being the guilty party. So, their defensive (reactive) behaviors will work against cooperation, break down relationships, create hurt feelings, and waste a lot of time and effort. They will also generate their own drama stories that will negatively impact them for some time afterward.

When you focus on the outcome, people are much less likely to feel threatened.

- They will see you as a partner as you work together toward solutions.
- They will gain some pride in being a part of the solution.
- Best of all, they will walk away from the experience feeling better about themselves and in a positive frame of mind.

The outcome you choose must be a *mutually beneficial outcome*—something that would be in the best interests for everyone involved. It's tempting to think of a self-centered goal focused on getting your own needs met. However, in order to Pivot to Power you need to take the role of creator. That means focusing on an outcome that is going to benefit all of the concerned parties. Not only will this produce a better overall outcome, it will enhance your relationships and increase the other party's willingness to cooperate in the future.

Akeela experienced this when her new boss, Ben, assigned her a project with a due date she could not meet because of her demanding workload. Her first reaction was to become angry and judgmental. She told herself, "This is proof Ben doesn't know what he is doing!" She caught herself though, and realized she felt persecuted by this unfair assignment that made her feel angry and resentful. She used the Tame It step to calm down and clear her head. She identified her need for fairness in establishing a reasonable workload. Then she focused on her outcome.

Initially, she wanted to avoid the assignment and find a way to tell Ben she couldn't do it and leave it at that. However, I prompted her to consider the outcomes for everyone in this matter. She realized her boss's need to get this project completed within a certain timeframe would not be addressed with that response. So instead, she chose to sit down and discuss it with him. She explained how other important priorities made it impossible for her to meet the assigned deadline. Then she brainstormed with him other ways to get the assignment accomplished. Because she knew the organization so much better than he, she was able to identify people who could get it done within the desired timeframe.

CHAPTER 13

She then talked with him about involving her to do workload planning *before* assigning a big project. He said he would be happy to do so. Ben expressed his gratitude and acknowledged his respect for the skillful way she handled the matter.

Identify what actually happened, the objective facts of the situation and challenge your assumptions. Drama stories are usually a far cry from what actually happened. Identifying the objective facts illuminates the false assumptions that gave rise to the drama story in the first place. And that makes it much easier to achieve a positive outcome.

Identifying the facts in a situation requires being able to describe the situation using *action language. You are using action language when you describe things that can be seen on a video recording of the scene.*

For instance, the statement, "He criticized me," cannot be seen on a video. The word "criticized" is the *label* given to the words actually spoken. What he actually said was, "I don't think you put enough time or effort into this report." And that *can* be seen on a video.

Following are some examples of incorrect and correct action language:

CORRECT	INCORRECT
He did not answer my question.	He ignored me.
Brent did not laugh at my joke.	Brent is in a bad mood.
She talked to other people but not to me in the elevator.	She's a snob.
The selection committee picked someone other than me to lead the project.	The selection process was not fair.
Sam sometimes talks in a loud voice when on phone calls.	Sam is an inconsiderate jerk.
Karim ate lunch at his desk.	Karim is a slob.
LaShonda missed today's soccer practice.	LaShonda doesn't care about the team.

The examples of incorrect statements are drama stories. The speaker's emotions are tied to those interpretations. When you read down the list on the right, you might find yourself reacting to some of those inflammatory labels even though they are completely fictitious scenarios. That's because you have triggers tied to some of those experiences as well. Have you ever been ignored, dealt with unfairly, or been treated like a second-class citizen?

This shared experience is one of the reasons you are so easily enrolled in other people's drama stories. You can relate to them.

CHAPTER 13

Now read the list of statements on the left. These statements use objective action language. No emotions are imbedded in those statements. Reading the list, you may be thinking to yourself, "So what? What's so bad about that?" because the facts of a situation are almost always emotionally neutral.

Describing the situation using action language can help reframe your interpretation of what happened.

- Action language makes it evident your emotions are about your story—your interpretation—and empowers you to take responsibility for it.
- It opens the door for you to question your assumptions about the situation: what the other party was thinking and feeling, what their intentions were, how other people viewed you, what the implications are for you, whether there is really a reason for concern.

Action language enables you to identify alternative explanations for the situation that are just as valid and much more empowering. For instance:

- Ask yourself if there is any evidence to contradict your conclusion. There's almost always other facts that you have omitted, ignored, or distorted that would support a more positive interpretation.
- Consider what else the situation might mean. Deliberately create empowering interpretations that open the door for a positive resolution.
- Give the other party the benefit of the doubt. If it had been you doing the behavior, you would have

a positive explanation for your actions—a positive intent. Grant the same to the other people in your situation.

See the situation from the other party's perspective, and then share yours. When you view a situation through the egocentric lens of your own BIAS, it's easy to villainize another party.

When considering another person's actions we often lament, "Why would they do that?" We imply something is wrong with them; they have no valid justification for their behavior. Of course, when *we* do those same behaviors, we think we are perfectly justified and the validity of our logic is crystal clear.

You may recall from our initial discussion of drama stories in Chapter 4 that persecutors don't think they have done anything wrong. They often claim the victim's action (or inaction) forced them to do what they did.

> When you view a situation through the egocentric lens of your own BIAS, it's easy to villainize another party.

You may not agree with other people's logic, but you have to admit they had reasons that were *valid for them* for what they did. That's the key. Their BIAS led to different choices than yours would have. Maybe they aren't *wrong*; maybe they're just *different*. We may strongly disagree with someone's BIAS and their choices, but that's a different kind of conversation than "what they did is wrong."

Taking the time to understand the situation from the other party's perspective—walking in their shoes—can

CHAPTER 13

help you to be more open minded and let go of your judgments. Hopefully, you will develop compassion for their experience.

Sometimes the other party's actions are considered "wrong" based on common social standards—stealing, having an affair, cheating, physically abusing someone, blatantly lying, and the like. Even under these circumstances, you can develop compassion when you try to understand the situation from their perspective. And that will lead to a more productive resolution than when you feel righteous justification in meting out punishment or retribution.

Remember, force begets more force.

To understand the other person's perspective, you repeat the Name It step from the other party's point of view. If possible, ask the other party to answer these questions. If not, answer them to the best of your ability from what you imagine the other party's answers would be. *You have to be as <u>generous</u> with your answers <u>for them</u> as you were with <u>yourself</u>.*

Questions to ask:

1. *How do you see this situation?* (their interpretation/story)

2. *How has this impacted you?* (how they have been thwarted, threatened, or hurt?)

3. *How are you feeling about this situation?* (their emotions)

4. *What do you need that you aren't getting?* (their underlying needs)

5. *What outcome do you want?* (their preferred solution to the problem)

Once you understand their perspective, use empathic listening to reflect back your understanding and validate their experience. This will help neutralize their emotional charge and increase their willingness to cooperate.

Notice how your deeper understanding of their perspective changes how you view the other party and the situation. Hopefully, you will feel empathy for their experience. When you allow yourself to be changed by the other person's point of view, the possibility of mutually beneficial outcomes will be dramatically increased.

> Your vulnerability opens the door for the other party to connect with you as a human being—to have empathy for your viewpoint

After you validate their experience, there's a natural invitation for you to share your perspective with the other party. Dr. Stephen Covey described this in his best-selling book *The 7 Habits of Highly Effective People* as "Seek *first* to understand, and *then* to be understood."

It's not enough to understand the other party, you need to be understood as well. Remember to take the high road! Share your point of view without judgmental language, without making anyone wrong, and by taking ownership for your thoughts, emotions, and actions. Be sure to include your own emotions and underlying needs.

Ask the other party to reflect back what you said to ensure you were understood.

CHAPTER 13

Your <u>vulnerability</u> opens the door for the other party to connect with you as a human being—to have empathy for your viewpoint. When both parties have empathy for one another, an empathic connection is created. And this paves the way for easier and more effective resolutions of situations to everyone's satisfaction.

The next chapter illustrates several applications of Max the Moment to help deepen your understanding of this life-changing life skill.

CHAPTER 14

Applying Max the Moment

Practice makes perfect. I recommend you practice Max the Moment multiple times every day until it becomes a habit. Soon it will become second nature and it will transform your life!

Following are two examples to illustrate using Max the Moment to Pivot to Power in the moment of an upset. The first is a fairly simple situation and the second far more complex and dramatic. The third example illustrates how to use Max the Moment strategically to evaluate a recurring pattern of reaction in order to prevent it in the future.

Example 1 — Missing an Important Meeting

Here's an example of how quick and easy the Max the Moment process can be. Imagine you are driving to work in morning rush hour traffic. You're looking forward to an important meeting to present the results of your project to senior management. You have just enough time to get to work, collect your thoughts, and then join the meeting.

Then you see the cars ahead of you come to a complete halt with no apparent explanation. As traffic crawls along and you watch the minutes tick by, you become more and more frustrated and angry with the traffic jam. That's when you need to practice Max the Moment.

Tame It. You realize you are upset with the situation because you are tensing up, starting to feel angry, and experiencing a lot of negative self-talk (like "What's the matter with you people? Move it!").

You say, "Stop!" in your mind and interrupt your inner dialogue.

You take a couple of minutes to just breathe through it and drain your emotions. You now feel much calmer and more level headed.

Name It. You own up to feeling victimized by the traffic jam and angry and frustrated that you may be late or even miss your meeting. A lot of important people have taken time out to be at this meeting, so a lot is at stake for you.

Your *need* is to show up well and do a great job with your presentation.

Reframe It. Then you focus on the *outcome* you want in this situation, which is to get to the meeting on time.

Given your need to be viewed in a positive light, you don't want to be the reason the meeting is postponed. Then you examine your assumptions about the consequences of rescheduling the meeting. You realize arriving extremely late or missing the meeting entirely while everyone else was there on time would be even worse.

CHAPTER 14

Even though it will be inconvenient for everyone, you decide to call ahead and simply reschedule the meeting. It's a better alternative than being late and wasting people's time. Your boss isn't happy about it but understands.

You continue to breathe deeply and practice mindfulness and eventually the traffic jam clears up. You arrive at work calm and relaxed and discover that two senior executives had also been caught in the traffic jam so the meeting had been canceled anyway!

Example 2 — Trying to Be "Superwoman"... and Failing

Here's a second and more complex application of the Max the Moment process. Early in our relationship, Akeela described how overwhelmed she felt trying to be everything to everyone—and to do it perfectly. This role of "superwoman" is one many of my female clients have struggled with, and maybe some of you can relate to it too.

Akeela and I had begun addressing the limiting beliefs, unrealistic expectations, and ineffective strategies in her BIAS regarding this pattern. Then Akeela had a meltdown, and subsequent breakthrough, that dramatically accelerated the clearing of this pattern. Here's the story she told me about how she used Max the Moment to create a liberating breakthrough in her "superwoman" pattern.

"Last week I worked later than usual for a Friday, and arrived home exhausted at about 9pm. My feet hurt, my back ached, and I was so fatigued that my head felt like it was stuffed with cotton. I just wanted to crawl into a steaming hot bath and soak for an hour before collapsing into bed.

When I entered the house, I was confronted with heaping piles of dirty clothes in the laundry room. I stopped in my tracks. I couldn't believe it. I expected Tom and the kids to finish washing and putting away the laundry before I got back home. They had nothing else to do all day because it was summer break, and yet there sat the laundry ... untouched. And then I walked into the kitchen.

Pots with food still in them were sitting on the stove. The sink was overflowing with unwashed dishes. And when I peeked into the dining room, I saw that the dishes and condiments from dinner were still on the table.

I looked into the living room and saw that Tom was watching sports and drinking a beer. He had not even noticed I was there. By this time, tears were pouring down my face, and I think I momentarily stopped breathing. After everything I did for them, they didn't have enough appreciation to even pick up after themselves ... leaving it to me to clean up after them.

I started to panic. I was thinking it was never going to stop ... the unbearable burden of this mountain of responsibilities was never going to let up. And I had nothing left in my tank to deal with it all. I started feeling desperate, sort of like a trapped animal. It felt like every cell of my body was screaming. This may sound strange, but in that moment it felt like a life and death situation ... I just couldn't go on that way anymore. I

CHAPTER 14

wanted to run away ... I backed away and out into the garage where I leaned over on the hood of the car, put my head down and cried my eyes out.

Tame It.

Once my crying slowed, I started to get angry ... no, I became furious! I felt an almost irresistible urge to walk in and sweep everything off the table onto the floor, pull the dishes out of the sink and start throwing them. I wanted to smash everything. That's when I realized how profoundly triggered I was. The negative thoughts, the raging anger ... I was nearly panting in my fury. And I realized I had to calm down.

I shouted, "STOP!!!!" in my mind ... and there was just this silence after that. I blanked my mind—quit thinking about anything—and started breathing long and slow and deep like we had practiced and I started to feel a little better.

Then I drained the pain. It took a while, but that helped a lot. But I was still upset, so I knew there was more. I felt good enough that I could go back into the house and not get triggered again. So I went in and climbed into a hot bath and laid back and relaxed. While I soaked, I consoled the part of me that was still upset—turns out there were three of them! One was feeling unappreciated and unloved, another was still angry, and the third was paralyzed with fear. I felt really calm and clear after that. I was too exhausted to do anything else so I just fell into bed and a deep dreamless sleep.

Name It.

The next morning, I waded through that messy kitchen, made coffee, and then went into the study and closed the door. I wanted private time to work through my drama story. Although it took a while, I eventually sorted it out.

At first, I thought Tom and the kids were the villains in my story. They were being irresponsible and lazy—expecting me to work all day to pay the bills then handle everything at home. But then I realized that these feelings go beyond the home and include work. I feel overwhelmed with everything I have on my plate at work too. And I have some of the same emotions: anger, resentment, self-pity, despair. I realized I was the common factor and that I had better look at how I'm contributing to the situation.

What I need is to take care of myself, and that will require me to scale back my responsibilities to a manageable level and get more support from others. I realized that I have a limiting belief that goes back to my childhood that I <u>should</u> be responsible and handle everything by myself. Being "the responsible one" seems to have become part of my identity. I will have to let go of that belief and also be willing to change some of my behaviors at work and home to enable a more balanced life. I also need to be willing to ask for—and receive—support from others. I know that won't be easy, but I'm ready now to make those changes!

Reframe It.

I thought about the outcomes I wanted given my need to take care of myself and create better life balance. At

CHAPTER 14

home, I wanted everyone to step up and take on more of the household chores. I also wanted to create some "me time"—to set time aside every week just for me to do whatever I wanted. At work, I wanted to reduce the number of items on my to-do list and set some boundaries about how much time I was willing to devote to work.

I called Tom, Sophie, and James together to talk—Zuri was on a weekend trip. I explained that I wanted to talk about my concerns. I told them how I felt when I got home and found that mess the night before. I even told them about my emotional meltdown and why I felt the way I did. Both the kids and Tom looked distraught that I had been so upset.

Then I stopped and asked them to tell me what had led to the clothes not getting washed and the kitchen not getting cleaned up. The kids looked surprised and explained that they thought I liked doing those things. They said I was always cleaning up and just assumed that I was happy doing it. They pointed out that when they tried to help, I often shooed them away or came along after them and redid the work they'd already done to get it the way I wanted it.

At first I was astonished they would think that, but then I realized that I did all those things the kids were pointing out. It seemed reasonable they could have concluded I would prefer to do it myself. I took the opportunity to explain that I did not, in fact, enjoy it and that we needed to work out a system so that everyone chipped in and helped out.

I asked Tom to explain about the laundry. He said he still planned to do it and was going to do it that day. He hadn't realized it was so important to me to get it done the day before. Tom showed real remorse and apologized profusely for upsetting me. I stopped him and said that the apology needed to be for not doing the laundry, not for upsetting me. I created the upset and I had taken ownership of it.

At this point, I asked for their ideas about how we could address my concerns regarding household maintenance, and we came up with some workable solutions. Among the many solutions we worked out was everyone agreeing to clean up after themselves, and the kids dividing up the kitchen duties for cleaning up after meals. Tom will continue to cook dinners, and has committed to doing his "chores" on specific days and times so he can plan ahead for them and I will know what to expect. For my part, I agreed to let them do things their way even if it is different from the way I would do it. (As a side note, I carried that learning over to my role as a manager at work!) Also, I am not going to be reminding anyone of their responsibilities—they have committed to reminding each other.

I am going to take several hours each weekend to do something just for me. I realized that when I take better care of myself, I will be able to be more loving toward my family and have more fun with them.

I'm delighted to say that so far it's working, and what a big relief it is! The funny thing about everyone helping out now is that the family is happier and we have drawn closer together. I didn't expect that, but I'm thrilled!

CHAPTER 14

Akeela's recovery from her self-described "emotional meltdown" was nothing short of heroic—an incredible display of courage and inner strength! And her use of Max the Moment was masterful.

- Despite being in full-blown emotional hijack, Akeela was able to recognize that she was triggered and start the process of recovery.
- She breathed deeply to help restore some clarity to her thinking and calm herself down. She used both the Drain the Pain and Console Yourself life skills to deflate the emotional charge and further restore power to her pilot.
- Then Akeela described her drama story and realized it was bigger than just her issues with the family. When she recognized the larger pattern, she could see more clearly her role in creating it.
- She identified her need, which is to take better care of herself. Then she focused on what outcome she wanted from the family.
- When she called them together, she didn't unload on them and shame them the way someone might who was still triggered. Instead, she told them the truth about her reaction. Then she gave them the space to share their point of view. To her credit, she was able to see their side of things and factor their points into the steps needed to address her concerns.
- Ultimately, the family developed a plan that works for everyone. Not only did it address Akeela's specific concern, it had a much bigger effect in bringing them closer together.

Akeela and I used this breakthrough to discuss changes she could make at work. She determined to limit her work hours to 10 hours per day and to free up her weekends from office work, except for rare circumstances. She set a goal of being home for dinner with the family when she wasn't traveling. She also committed to getting at least 7 hours of sleep each night.

She delegated some responsibilities and took a more hands-off approach by letting her team come up with their own solutions, even if it was different from how she would have done it. Akeela negotiated her priorities with her boss to get some projects off her plate and others put on the back burner. She also learned to say no to new requests if she really didn't have the capacity for them. She focused more and didn't waste time on unimportant matters. Managing her email better saved her more time than she expected. And being very discerning about which meetings needed her attendance freed up a lot more time.

Akeela discovered what everyone who makes these kinds of changes eventually learns. She works less but gets more done and with higher quality. She feels better and has more energy and that leads to being happier and feeling less pressure. She is more creative, has more time for strategic thinking and for developing her people. And best of all, her family life has improved a lot now that she is able to be more involved with the family.

This is certainly one of the more extreme cases you would encounter for using Max the Moment. However, I wanted you to see how it works even under such challenging circumstances.

CHAPTER 14

Akeela's handling of her meltdown was infinitely better than the way I handled my "dark night of the soul" that I described in Chapter 1. At my low point in that process, I remember standing in my bathroom staring at that terrified man in the mirror and screaming at my reflection until I was hoarse. I screamed things like "What's wrong with you? You're worthless! Get your act together!" and I cursed myself for my failings and inadequacies. I pleaded with God for help and cried in despair standing in that empty house shrouded in loneliness, isolation, and hopelessness. I wish I had had these mindsets and life skills back then to help me through my crisis the way they helped Akeela.

It sometimes takes a complete meltdown to have a breakthrough. My breakdown was a crisis of identity, but others' breakdowns might be experienced as a heart attack from stress and overwork, a mid-life crisis, an affair, binge drinking that gets out of hand, or having their family walk out on them because they emotionally abandoned their family long ago.

Have you ever had a meltdown or breakdown similar to these? Do you ever feel like you're barely holding it together—that with the way things are going in your life you may be headed for a meltdown?

It sometimes takes a complete meltdown to have a breakthrough.

I think you might be surprised how many people share these feelings and experiences, which is one of the reasons why Inner Mastery is so important for transforming our lives. You don't have to get to a crisis state to take charge of your life. Speaking from experience, it is *much* better to take the gentle and easy route of Inner Mastery!

Escaping Your Personal "Groundhog Day"

In the movie *Groundhog Day*, Bill Murray's character, Phil Conners, finds himself living the same day over and over again. This continues for a painfully long period of time until he makes some fundamental changes and gains far greater emotional maturity. Then through these new thoughts and behaviors, he breaks the pattern and ends the cycle. He is thrilled the morning he awakes and it's literally a new day for him.

Many of us have similar experiences with our emotional reactions. Like our own personal Groundhog Day, these reactions repeat over and over again—the same reaction just in different circumstances. We are trapped in an unending cycle, reliving our past in the present day.

You can use Max the Moment to break yourself out of those reactive patterns.

Start with identifying your most common emotional upsets. Upon reflection, you will likely be able to identify anywhere from three to six recurring upsets you experience frequently and in many different circumstances. If you struggle to identify yours, you can ask the people close to you for their input. You might also take a week or two to just pay attention to when, why, and how you get upset and keep track of the incidents. Your patterns will soon become evident.

CHAPTER 14

Your upsets don't have to be visible to other people. Internalized upsets are just as concerning as those you act out publicly. Your psychological and physiological consequences are the same. Internal upsets simply have less impact on others. But even then, other people are almost guaranteed to notice by certain verbal and body language clues that you are triggered.

> Like our own personal Groundhog Day, everyone has reactions that repeat over and over again—the same reaction just in different circumstances. We are trapped in an unending cycle, reliving our past in the present day.

Once you have pinpointed your most common reactions, use Max the Moment to analyze how to break these patterns. Set aside some time and work through each step of the process for each pattern. Work the process as if the reaction were happening in the present moment, but in super slow motion. Slowing it all down enables you to gain a lot more clarity and detail about your inner experience. It also helps in constructing productive responses for your triggers.

This approach has one additional step. For your recurring patterns, it is important to develop a power phrase to help you anchor in the desired changes.

Akeela did this exercise and identified the following situations that consistently caused her to react in a negative manner:

1. Not being acknowledged for her ability or recognized for her accomplishments

2. Being criticized or unfairly blamed for something
3. Being overly responsible—trying to be everything to everyone and neglecting her own needs
4. Needing to win—to look good and especially to be right about everything

Example 3 —Preventing Recurring Patterns of Behavior

Akeela experienced a recent situation that involved the second of these patterns, being unfairly blamed. So we decided to use it as our example to work through this process.

<u>The Situation</u>: Akeela's new boss, Ben, called a meeting to discuss an issue regarding one of the company's key customers. The meeting included Akeela and her peers as well as key people from other parts of the company.

Akeela wisely and calmly prepared for the meeting as we discussed. She reflected on the task outcomes she wanted, which were to solve the customer's issue and make any needed process improvements. She also developed a relationship goal to be supportive with everyone involved and partner with others to achieve the goal.

As the meeting progressed, Akeela's peer, Carlos, blamed her and her team for an incorrect analysis that was costly for the customer. Ben hastily agreed and told her to fix it. Akeela felt attacked and immediately went into one of her habitual reactions. She knew her analysis had been correct and felt Ben was an idiot for not seeing

CHAPTER 14

her viewpoint. Akeela was seething internally, but tried not to show it. However, her peers reported later that she was highly defensive and her anger showed through in her tone of voice and body language.

After the meeting, Akeela set out to vindicate herself and her team. They reviewed the analysis and all of the supporting details and were able to prove the cause of the issue actually lay in Carlos's department. His department used an older, outdated version of Akeela's team's analysis even though they were given the updated version. Carlos had been outspoken in his criticism of her and her team in the meeting, and she couldn't wait to get payback.

Akeela called a meeting with Ben and Carlos and laid out the evidence that showed it was actually Carlos's team's fault and not her own. Sadly, the meeting didn't go as planned. Ben was annoyed with her and criticized her for not focusing on solving the issue and for blaming and finger pointing. Then Ben reprimanded Carlos for not taking more care and for using the incorrect analysis. Ben was disappointed in her, and Carlos was now angry and resentful toward her.

This situation reflected poorly on everyone involved. Ben didn't take the time to get the facts, and took a blaming approach rather than a solution orientation. Carlos criticized Akeela in the meeting and then acted like a victim when his team was found to be at fault. Akeela mishandled the situation all the way around. She became a victim in the first meeting and handled the situation poorly, and then became the persecutor in the second meeting where she alienated Ben and Carlos.

These types of consequences are typical when you allow your autopilot reactions to run the show. Akeela failed to get her outcome and also put herself in a hole in her relationships with her boss and peer.

As humans, no matter how much we practice breathing, remaining calm, and draining the pain, there will be times when our emotions are still triggered. You may think Akeela reverted backward to step one, but the truth is she continues improving. Our goal is progress, not perfection.

In this instance, she felt attacked and responded defensively. Remaining calm in the face of an attack takes practice, but you can turn it around. You'll discover a big difference below in how she applied Max the Moment to release her feelings and resolve the situation with Carlos.

Overview of Applying Max the Moment

1) Tame It — Akeela reflected on the situation as if it were in the present. I asked her to recall the moment she was accused of making a mistake. I asked, "What were the cues you were going into a drama story and becoming emotionally upset?"

She replied, "I was clenching my teeth, my cheeks were feeling flushed, and I felt a big knot in my gut like a fist. At first I felt angry and frustrated, and later starting feeling resentful."

Simply remembering the incident was causing Akeela to relive the emotional reaction all over again. That's the nature of drama stories—the subconscious thinks the

CHAPTER 14

memory is happening in the present moment and you relive the upset again.

Her inner dialogue was quite revealing of her upset. Regarding her boss, she said to herself, "This is ridiculous! He doesn't know what he is talking about." With her peer it was "You jerk! I can't believe you are piling on like that and after I covered for you so many times. You're going to regret this ... just wait until the next time you need my help to bail you out of a mess!"

> As humans, no matter how much we practice breathing, remaining calm, and draining the pain, there will be times when our emotions are still triggered. Our goal is progress, not perfection.

I could tell she was embarrassed to admit those thoughts. I validated her saying, "Those are normal feelings. I completely understand and I am not judging you for having them. I want to acknowledge you for the courage and humility it took to admit those negative thoughts. By speaking up like you did, you have the possibility to make a much bigger shift than if you had tried to hide them and sugarcoat what really happened for you."

I asked Akeela to notice where in her body she felt the emotions, and suggested she look for places with pressure or tension. Some resided in her throat, heart, and gut areas.

I sat quietly and watched as she closed her eyes and turned her attention inward as she began to Drain the Pain. She took several deep cleansing breaths and then sat motionless. I could see a visible change as she completed releasing the emotions in each of the three areas. She physically relaxed and her skin tone showed more color and appeared healthier. She let out a long breath and her shoulders slumped a bit more as she released more and more tension.

When she was done, I asked her, "How do you feel now?" She laughed and said, "I feel really light and kinda open ... like my heart is more open or something. When I first opened my eyes, it was like everything was brighter and the colors were more vivid. It was strange, but really wonderful!" And she laughed again. I asked her about the laughter, and she explained, "I just feel really light-hearted ... just very relieved. I feel happier, more hopeful and optimistic."

2) Name It — I asked Akeela to dig deeper regarding the emotions she experienced, "What emotions are underneath the anger and frustration? Is there something else going on at a deeper level?" She stopped and I could see her thinking about it. She seemed to struggle with the question. After a couple of minutes she answered, "I felt humiliated and ashamed ... and then I heard a small voice deep within speaking in fear ... that I had done something wrong and displeased someone important."

Akeela sat silently for a few moments as she considered that insight. She said, "It feels strangely liberating to be able to admit it out loud." And then she laughed again and actually looked like a weight had been lifted from her.

I asked her to describe the drama story that hooked her emotionally. Akeela could clearly see how Ben and later her peers were persecutors and she was the victim. Ben was unfairly blaming her for something that wasn't her fault. She felt her peers were "throwing her under the

CHAPTER 14

bus," that she was being scapegoated and made to look bad in front of her boss.

She struggled to identify her needs in this situation. So, I asked her what she wanted to experience that was missing for her. After reflecting on this, she replied, "I think it's safety, and also maybe justice."

Akeela's *need* was safety—to protect herself and her team from inaccurate information and accusations, and also to know justice would be served and the misunderstanding would be cleared up. Because she felt humiliated and ashamed in this situation, she had overreacted and taken a vengeful approach—hurting herself and others in the process. And, ironically, creating even greater feelings of humiliation and shame.

3) Reframe It — I asked Akeela, "What would you do differently if you could replay the scene in a more productive and effective way?"

Akeela noted several outcomes she wanted from the meeting.

- She wanted to make sure they were dealing with facts and not opinions so they could make a valid assessment of the situation.
- She wanted to focus on the desired outcome, which was to make the customer happy and to improve the process that had caused the issue.
- She also wanted to make sure nobody felt attacked or blamed—she wanted to partner with people so they could focus on the solution and not spend time and energy avoiding blame.

I asked her to describe what the challenge was for her personally—what made it impossible to achieve those outcomes in the original meeting? She answered immediately, "I need to stop taking it personally when people find fault with me or my team. I want to let go of the need to look good all the time, and especially to let go of my need to be right."

I wondered aloud, "How are you going to do that in the future?" Akeela sat in silence thinking about her answer. Then she said, "I'm aware of the pattern now, and I'm going to notice immediately when I'm getting triggered and work Max the Moment. Then I'll take responsibility by saying something like, 'If my team made a mistake, we want to know about it so we can take steps to make it right.' Then I want to focus the group on the desired outcome. I'll ask non-threatening questions to help surface the facts and especially to separate fact from opinion. I want to focus the meeting on the tangible actions we can take to improve the situation. Then get firm commitments on who is going to do what. Throughout the process, I want to be supportive of the people in the room."

I thought her assessment was excellent! But as Cervantes said, "The proof of the pudding is in the eating." So we would have to wait and see what happened the next time Akeela felt similarly challenged.

4) Develop a Power Phrase for This Situation — To wrap up this process, I asked Akeela to identify one or more power phrases that would capture the essence of this Pivot to Power for her.

CHAPTER 14

She tried out several different ideas, and then settled on the phrases: "This is not personal," and "Focus on the outcome." In the future, once she recognizes the pattern is being triggered, she can mentally repeat her power phrases to help her refocus. These will act like new triggers and automatically shift her emotional and mental state toward the productive outcome she outlined above.

<u>Postscript</u>: At my urging, Akeela met with her peer from this situation to make amends. She reported that she started off by giving Carlos some time to vent about how he felt about the whole affair. He started off by attacking her personally and blaming her for the situation. So, Akeela focused on breathing and draining the pain as her emotions were triggered by his attacks. Akeela also used the power phrase: "This is not about me; it's his pain speaking. Just focus on the outcome," to help her stay out of drama. She knew this was his drama and she kept in mind another power phrase, "This is not my circus, not my monkeys."

When Carlos finished, Akeela used empathic listening to reflect back to him what his experience had been. She said Carlos looked somewhat astonished but said, "Yeah, that's right." He relaxed a lot and the tension went out of his face and shoulders.

Then Akeela apologized for her reaction. She admitted what she had done, how it had impacted him, and that she was really sorry. She committed to partnering with him in the future.

Carlos looked at her in disbelief at her unexpected behavior and then simply said, "Thank you." He seemed at a loss for words.

Akeela then described what she had experienced when Carlos had blamed Akeela and her team. She said, "I heard you say my team was to blame for this issue, and when I followed up, you could not provide any supporting data. I felt angry because I was accused of something without any evidence it was valid. What I needed was to be treated fairly and to protect my team's integrity in this situation. I request that you avoid assigning blame in the future and partner with me to explore the facts with an eye toward solving the problem."

Then she asked Carlos to reflect back what she had said. Akeela stepped in and made a couple of corrections but then was satisfied with his response.

Then she initiated a partnering conversation. She asked Carlos to explore with her what they could both do differently in the future to be more supportive of one another in similar situations. She explained to me the ideas they discussed and felt the meeting had gone a long way toward transforming their relationship.

I was thrilled! She took the initiative and demonstrated tremendous resourcefulness in transforming a damaged relationship into a much more supportive and cooperative one.

That is what Inner Mastery looks like!

EPILOGUE

Your Ongoing Journey of Inner Mastery

I hope you are already seeing amazing changes in your life through the insights and strategies you have explored in these pages! Making these skills and perspectives an integral part of your life requires practice, practice, practice! View your world through these mindsets and practice the life skills every day and they will soon become second nature.

There is so much more information and help available to you as you continue your journey of Inner Mastery! Your first step has been self-awareness and emotional self-management, which has been the focus of this book. However, achieving Inner Mastery involves so much more than this, including:

- Knowing and identifying with your True Self rather than your ego
- Identifying and healing your deep insecurities—your negative self-beliefs

- Embracing your "shadow" side—the parts of you that you don't want to admit are there or that you are ashamed of
- Learning to tune into and follow your inner guidance and to have a personal relationship with your Higher Self
- Releasing judgment, criticism, and comparisons that alienate you from others, and choosing compassion and acceptance instead
- Being able to recognize and align yourself with your own life path, and discovering how to cooperate rather than compete with life—to "go with the flow"
- Developing wisdom—putting things into a larger perspective and seeing the interconnectedness of life

Dear Human: Master Your Emotions is the first book in the Inner Mastery series. Look for upcoming "Dear Human" books, which will address the topics above and more. Be sure to check out the free resources available at www.MasterYourEmotionsBook.com. These include:

- Study guides for book clubs, couples, etc.
- Downloadable versions of the key graphics in this book
- Additional insights on our blog, and much more!

I also want to encourage you to visit the Inner Mastery Community at www.InnerMasteryCommunity.com. This community is designed to support your basic human need

EPILOGUE

for connection, being seen and accepted for who you are, for spiritual growth, emotional and mental healing, and your ongoing quest to be your best self.

Learning to be in community with others is one of the essential life skills our society so dearly needs. You will have the opportunity to join a small "circle" of people who will provide friendship, support, and loving acceptance. Here, you can be your authentic and messy self without concern for being judged or questioned for your thoughts, actions, or emotions. Your circle of friends will support and encourage you to rise up to meet and transcend your challenges, and to fulfill your potential. And you will be able to support them in return.

> *Learning to be in community with others is one of the essential life skills our society so dearly needs.*

Your journey is further enriched through a large and ever-growing library of multi-media learning modules on the many dimensions of Inner Mastery. All of which are available as part of your membership.

Let's continue the conversation we started with this book! Come join us in the Inner Mastery Community and let's keep exploring how your life can keep getting better and better. I want to get to know you better, explore your questions, and share the joy of learning and growing together in a loving and supportive community. I look forward to seeing you there!

ABOUT THE AUTHOR

Mark Youngblood is a lifelong student, and for the past two decades a teacher and facilitator of Inner Mastery. Mark's purpose in life is to elevate human consciousness and promote spiritual growth, individually and collectively. He founded his company, Inner Mastery, Inc., 20+ years ago to promote personal and organizational transformation. His outreach presently includes executive coaching with top management, the Inner Mastery Learning Community, the Dear Human series of books, public speaking, workshops, and life coaching.

Mark began his career as a Certified Public Accountant and it took him about 18 minutes to realize this path did not appeal to him. After a few years, he transitioned into consulting to implement enterprise-wide software systems and lead large-scale organizational change efforts. He then transitioned into transformational coaching, which he has been practicing for nearly two decades. He is a Master Practitioner and Trainer of Neuro-Linguistic Programming and has read, studied, and practiced extensively in the art and science of personal transformation and spiritual growth. His previous books are *Eating the*

Chocolate Elephant: Take Charge of Change, and *Life at the Edge of Chaos: Creating the Quantum Organization*.

Mark is a proud father and stepfather and is married to his high school sweetheart who he reconnected with 35 years after their initial relationship ended. He is an avid traveler, a singer/songwriter, and a professional fine art photographer. You can view and purchase his artwork at www.MarkYoungblood.photos.

Related websites:

www.MyInnerMastery.com

www.DearHumanBooks.com

www.MasterYourEmotionsBook.com

www.InnerMasteryCommunity.com

SOURCES

Chapter 3

We who lived in – Frankl, *Man's Search for Meaning*, 75.

Chapter 4

Our brains take about 100 milliseconds — https://www.psychologytoday.com/blog/hold-me-tight/201004/suppressing-emotions

Chapter 5

We are not troubled — Epictetus as quoted in Fields et. al, *Chop Wood, Carry Water*, 182.

The Innocence Project reports — http://www.scientificamerican.com/article/do-the-eyes-have-it/

A full third of those — http://agora.stanford.edu/sjls/Issue%20One/fisher&tversky.htm

more akin to putting — http://www.scientificamerican.com/article/do-the-eyes-have-it/

Chapter 6

the only feeling that was approved of – *Parade* magazine, June 14, 2016, Page 12

Chapter 7

70% of adults – Bob Anderson, *Mastering Leadership*, "The Spirit of Leadership," Page 8

Research indicates 40 million people -- http://consumer.healthday.com/mental-health-information-25/addiction-news-6/40-million-americans-addicted-to-cigarettes-alcohol-or-drugs-666101.html

One in ten people — http://www.drugfree.org/new-data-show-millions-of-americans-with-alcohol-and-drug-addiction-could-benefit-from-health-care-r/

An astounding 52 million people - https://www.drugabuse.gov/related-topics/trends-statistics/infographics/popping-pills-prescription-drug-abuse-in-america

Nearly 12 million people — https://www.aamft.org/iMIS15/AAMFT/Content/consumer_updates/sexual_addiction.aspx

and from 5-7 percent — http://www.citizenlink.com/2010/06/14/frequently-asked-questions-gambling-in-the-united-states/

I found it quite surprising — http://news.sciencemag.org/brain-behavior/2014/07/people-would-rather-be-electrically-shocked-left-alone-their-thoughts

Chapter 8

The actual amount – Sohms and Turnbull, *The Brain and the Inner World*, 84

Chapter 9

Mindfulness has many benefits – http://www.apa.org/monitor/2012/07-08/ce-corner.aspx

A 2012 American Psychological Association study — http://www.forbes.com/sites/work-in-progress/2012/08/02/stress-at-work-is-bunk-for-business/

That's not so hard to imagine — http://www.forbes.com/sites/work-in-progress/2012/08/02/stress-at-work-is-bunk-for-business/

the acknowledgement of the positive — http://www.gratefulness.org/resource/what-is-gratitude/

People can't multitask very well — http://www.npr.org/templates/story/story.php?storyId=95256794

Inc. magazine reports — http://www.inc.com/laura-montini/infographic/the-high-cost-of-multitasking.html

Chapter 11

Fast Company Magazine reported — http://www.fastcompany.com/3032351/the-future-of-work/why-venting-about-work-actually-makes-you-angrier

This is the reason a crying baby — http://www.nytimes.com/1989/03/28/science/researchers-trace-empathy-s-roots-to-infancy.html?pagewanted=all

The health risks increase — http://www.huffingtonpost.ca/timi-gustafson/bottling-up-negative-emotions_b_5056433.html

www.ingramcontent.com/pod-product-compliance
Lightning Source LLC
Chambersburg PA
CBHW071659090426
42738CB00009B/1585